GREEN ISLES, BLUE WATERS, KIWI WONDERS

Green Isles, Blue Waters, Kiwi Wonders

ALINA HAZEL

Spectra Enterprise

CONTENTS

Table of Content

1

Introduction

3

Chapter 1

6

Chapter 2

16

Chapter 3

29

Chapter 4

41

Chapter 5

56

Chapter 6

69

Chapter 7

82

Chapter 8

95

Chapter 9

111

TABLE OF CONTENT

Introduction

Chapter 1: "Land of the Kiwi"

1.1 Introduction to New Zealand's unique nickname, "Land of the Kiwi."

1.2 Explore the symbolism of the kiwi bird and its representation of New Zealand's natural wonders.

1.3 Brief overview of the diverse landscapes and cultures in Aotearoa.

Chapter 2: "Nature's Canvas"

2.1 Dive into the breathtaking landscapes, from the lush greenery of Fiordland to the snow-capped peaks of the Southern Alps.

2.2 Explore the geothermal wonders of Rotorua and the volcanic landscapes that shape the North Island.

2.3 Highlight the significance of New Zealand's flora and fauna in shaping its natural beauty.

Chapter 3: "Blue Waters Beckon"

3.1 Discover the pristine blue waters surrounding New Zealand, from the Tasman Sea to the Pacific Ocean.

3.2 Explore the marine life, including whales, dolphins, and the unique yellow-eyed penguins.

3.3 Discuss the importance of sustainable marine practices and conservation efforts.

Chapter 4: "Maori Myths and Legends"

4.1 Delve into the rich cultural heritage of the Maori people.

4.2 Explore traditional myths and legends that are woven into the landscape and landmarks.

4.3 Discuss the importance of the Maori language (Te Reo) and the preservation of cultural traditions.

Chapter 5: "Adventure Awaits"

5.1 Highlight New Zealand's reputation as the adventure capital of the world.

5.2 Explore activities such as bungee jumping, skydiving, and hiking in the spectacular landscapes.

5.3 Discuss the balance between adventure tourism and environmental conservation.

Chapter 6: "Kiwi Hospitality"

6.1 Explore the warm and welcoming nature of the Kiwi people.

6.2 Discuss the importance of hospitality in New Zealand culture.

6.3 Share stories of travelers' experiences and connections with locals.

Chapter 7: "Culinary Delights"

7.1 Explore New Zealand's unique culinary scene, featuring fresh and local ingredients.

7.2 Highlight traditional Maori cuisine and the fusion of international influences.

7.3 Discuss the role of food in connecting with the culture and history of the region.

Chapter 8: "Conservation Chronicles"

8.1 Discuss New Zealand's commitment to environmental conservation.

8.2 Explore initiatives to protect native species and restore ecosystems.

8.3 Highlight success stories and ongoing challenges in conservation efforts.

Chapter 9: "A Kiwi's Journey"

9.1 Conclude the book with a reflection on the author's personal journey through the Green Isles and Blue Waters of New Zealand.

9.2 Encourage readers to embark on their own adventures and explore the wonders of Aotearoa.

9.3 Provide practical tips for travelers, including sustainable practices and cultural sensitivity.

INTRODUCTION

In the southwestern Pacific Sea lies a domain of normal quality, social lavishness, and unrestrained experience — the spellbinding archipelago known as New Zealand. Suitably nicknamed the "Place that is known for the Kiwi," this island country entices with its lavish scenes, sky blue waters, and an embroidery of miracles that unfurl like a show-stopper painted essentially herself. In the accompanying investigation, we set out on an excursion through the verdant Green Isles, sail the tranquil Blue Waters, and dive into the heap Kiwi Ponders that characterize this captivating corner of the world.

New Zealand, or Aotearoa in the Maori language, is a country that blows some minds every step of the way. The moniker "Green Isles" gives recognition to the rich embroidery of vegetation that covers the islands, making a scene that appears to be practically powerful in its variety. From the snow-covered pinnacles of the Southern Alps to the calm rainforests of Fiordland, every last trace of the islands is a demonstration of the stunning magnificence of immaculate nature.

The material of New Zealand is painted with shades of green that reach from the energetic foliage of local trees like the kahikatea and totara to the rambling glades where sheep brush cheerily. This kaleidoscope of vegetation isn't just a setting however a vital piece of the Kiwi personality, molding the personality of the land and its kin. It is an update that in Aotearoa, nature is certainly not a different substance yet a no nonsense presence that illuminates each perspective regarding life.

Wandering past the verdant scenes, our look goes to the including Blue Waters that encompass the islands. The Tasman Ocean toward the west and the Pacific Sea toward the east support New Zealand in a marine hug, offering staggering vistas as well as a rich embroidery of marine life. The sky blue profundities are overflowing with dolphins that nimbly surf the waves, whales that break the surface in grand showcases, and provinces of penguins that waddle along the shores.

The part of "Blue Waters Call" is a demonstration of the significant association New Zealanders share with the ocean — a relationship that reaches out past entertainment to protection. The preservation endeavors pointed toward safeguarding marine biological systems and protecting the natural surroundings of jeopardized species uncover a guarantee to maintainability that reverberations all through the Kiwi way to deal with ecological stewardship.

As we drench ourselves in the regular ponders, our process takes us past the actual scenes to the domain of fantasy and legend. The Maori public, the native Polynesian occupants of New Zealand, have woven a rich embroidery of fantasies and legends that are indistinguishable from the actual texture of the islands. In "Maori Fantasies and Legends," we dig into the oral customs went down through ages, stories that talk about divine beings and goddesses forming the land, and stories that pervade geological highlights with social importance.

The Maori language, Te Reo, isn't just a method for correspondence yet a vessel for social personality and legacy. In the part of "Maori Fantasies and Legends," we investigate how the conservation of language turns into a course for the transmission of conventional information and a scaffold among over a significant time span. It is through the comprehension of these fantasies that the scene changes from a simple background to a no nonsense element with stories to tell.

No investigation of New Zealand would be finished without embracing the soul of experience that courses through its veins. "Experience Is standing by" as we cross the adrenaline-injected landscape, where the excitement of bungee leaping off abrupt precipices rivals the quietness of climbing through perfect public parks. New Zealand has legitimately procured its standing as the experience capital of the world, offering a jungle gym for daredevils and nature darlings the same.

However, in the midst of the elation, lies an upright way to deal with saving the fragile harmony between human diversion and the safeguarding of regular environments. The part of "Experience Is standing by" investigates the heartbeating exercises as well as the capable the travel industry rehearses that defend the very conditions that allure swashbucklers from around the globe.

Underneath the rush and fervor, the core of New Zealand beats with a glow and neighborliness that characterizes the Kiwi lifestyle. "Kiwi Cordiality" digs into the exceptional appeal of local people, known for their kind disposition and inviting nature. Whether tasting a level white in a Wellington bistro or taking part in a hongi (conventional Maori welcoming), guests end up embraced by a feeling of having a place that rises above social contrasts.

This glow stretches out to the culinary scene of New Zealand, a combination of flavors that reflects the social variety of its kin. "Culinary Joys" welcomes us to relish the extraordinary dishes that mix Maori customs with global impacts, exhibiting the homestead to-table ethos that portrays Kiwi cooking. From the customary hangi banquet to the tasty fish collected from immaculate waters, each nibble recounts an account of the land and its kin.

However, in the midst of the marvels and neighborliness, New Zealand isn't without its difficulties. The section of "Preservation Narratives" reveals insight into the ecological obstacles the country faces, from intrusive species compromising local verdure to the effect of environmental change on delicate biological systems. Through accounts of strength and preservation endeavors, we witness a country at the very front of supportable works on, endeavoring to be a steward of the climate for a long time into the future.

As we approach the finish of our excursion, "A Kiwi's Excursion" welcomes reflection on the individual encounters and revelations made en route. It is a source of inspiration for perusers to leave on their own investigation of the Green Isles, Blue Waters, and Kiwi Miracles. Reasonable tips for dependable travel and social responsiveness guide future explorers as they set off on a mission to uncover the fortunes that anticipate in this enamoring corner of the world.

CHAPTER 1

"Land of the Kiwi"

The Place where there is the Kiwi, a moniker that warmly typifies the quintessence of New Zealand, entices explorers with its unmatched excellence, rich social legacy, and different scenes that reach from immaculate sea shores to grand mountain ranges. This island country, arranged in the southwestern Pacific Sea, is prestigious for its one of a kind widely varied vegetation, represented most conspicuously by the kiwi bird - a flightless, nighttime avian species and a treasured symbol of the country.

New Zealand's North and South Islands, the two fundamental expanses of land that contain this captivating domain, offer an embroidery of regular ponders that unfurl as one sets out on an excursion of investigation. The North Island, with its geothermal wonders and cosmopolitan urban areas, remains as a conspicuous difference toward the South Island's rough fjords and snow-covered tops. The variety inside this generally little nation is astonishing, furnishing guests with a variety of encounters that mirror the range of regular magnificence.

The kiwi, New Zealand's informal image, isn't simply a bird yet a delegate of the country's remarkable personality. Endemic to these islands, the kiwi is a flightless bird with particular highlights, including a long snout and a layer of shaggy earthy colored feathers.

Eminent for its nighttime propensities, the kiwi is a tricky animal, making it an interesting and pursued sight for the two local people and vacationers the same. Preservation endeavors have been fundamental to saving this notorious species, with asylums and drives pointed toward safeguarding the kiwi and its environment.

Past the avian miracles, New Zealand is inseparable from its stunning scenes. The Fiordland Public Park, settled in the southwestern corner of the South Island, is a demonstration of the country's normal loftiness. Inlets, cut by ice sheets over hundreds of years, stretch like twisted strips between transcending precipices, making a powerful air. Milford Sound, a gem inside Fiordland, dazzles with its flowing cascades, reflect like waters, and the sensational pinnacles of Miter Pinnacle that penetrate the sky. The South Island's Southern Alps, a mountain range that traverses the length of the island, flaunts Aoraki/Mount Cook, New Zealand's most elevated top, encompassed by a snow capped scene of ice sheets and turquoise lakes.

In the interim, the North Island discloses its own miracles, eminently the geothermal wonders based on Rotorua. Pockets of fountains, natural aquifers, and percolating mud pools accentuate the scene, making an extraordinary climate. The Pohutu Fountain, in Te Whakarewarewa Warm Valley, captures everyone's attention with its strong ejections, arriving at noteworthy levels and leaving observers in stunningness of nature's crude power. The juxtaposition of these geothermal highlights against the rich vegetation of the encompassing backwoods establishes a dreamlike and charming climate one of a kind to New Zealand.

The Maori, the native individuals of New Zealand, inject the country with a rich social embroidery that is woven into the actual texture of its character. The haka, a conventional Maori war dance, is a strong and famous articulation of Maori culture, frequently performed to convey strength, solidarity, and regard. Carvings, known as Whakairo, embellish meeting houses and designs, portraying hereditary stories and profound associations with the land. Marae, customary gathering grounds, act as communities for mutual social events and festivities, where the Maori feature their well established customs through tune, dance, and the sharing of tribal accounts.

The appeal of New Zealand stretches out past its normal and social miracles to incorporate experience sports that draw adrenaline junkies from around the globe. Queenstown, settled on the shores of Lake Wakatipu in the South Island, is eminent as the "Experience Capital of the World." Here, adrenaline devotees can participate in exercises, for example, bungee hopping, skydiving, and stream drifting against a background of staggering high landscape. The rough scenes, sweeping fjords, and unblemished sea shores give a material to open air exercises going from climbing and skiing to water sports, taking special care of different interests and expertise levels.

New Zealand's obligation to natural manageability and preservation is clear in its public parks, marine stores, and drives pointed toward safeguarding the country's extraordinary biodiversity. The Branch of Protection (DOC) assumes an essential part in dealing with these region, guaranteeing that people in the future can keep on wondering about the country's regular miracles. From the unblemished sea shores of Abel Tasman Public Park to the snow capped knolls of Tongariro Public Park, each safeguarded region adds to the protection of New Zealand's environmental variety.

The Place that is known for the Kiwi remains as a demonstration of the amicable conjunction of spectacular scenes, social lavishness, and a promise to natural stewardship. New Zealand's character is complicatedly woven into the embroidery of its native legacy, represented by the kiwi and typified in the customs of the Maori public. As explorers adventure across the North and South Islands, they are blessed to receive a tangible gala of regular marvels, from the geothermal scenes of Rotorua to the glorious fjords of Fiordland. Experience coaxes every step of the way, and a significant regard for the climate saturates the nation's ethos. The Place where there is the Kiwi welcomes all who visit to set out on an excursion of revelation, appreciation, and association with a domain that really remains as one of the world's most remarkable objections.

1.1 Introduction to New Zealand's unique nickname, "Land of the Kiwi."

The moniker "Place that is known for the Kiwi" resounds profoundly with the novel character of New Zealand, catching the pith of this island country in the southwestern Pacific Sea. This moniker isn't only an eccentric mark; it is an emblematic portrayal of the country's normal fortunes, social lavishness, and a particular untamed life insignia — the kiwi bird. As we leave on an investigation of why New Zealand is lovingly called the "Place that is known for the Kiwi," we dive into the entwining accounts of its native legacy, biodiversity, and the preservation endeavors that feature the meaning of this charming epithet.

The Kiwi, a flightless, nighttime bird native to New Zealand, has turned into a notorious image profoundly implanted in the country's cognizance. With its long nose, shaggy earthy colored feathers, and an unmistakable, round body, the kiwi isn't simply an animal of the wild yet a magnetic representative for the country's one of a kind normal legacy. The association between the kiwi and New Zealand is significant to the point that the bird's name has been taken on to portray both individuals and the personality of the actual country.

The kiwi's nighttime propensities and slippery nature make it an uncommon sight in the wild, adding a quality of secret and selectiveness to its presence. Despite the fact that there are a few types of kiwi, including the notorious North Island kiwi (Apteryx mantelli), the Little Spotted Kiwi (Apteryx owenii), and others, they share normal qualities that recognize them collectively. The kiwi's dependence on its sharp feeling of smell and long, examining bill to search for bugs in the backwoods floor is a demonstration of its transformation to the remarkable biological systems of New Zealand.

The kiwi's importance reaches out past its portrayal in the normal world. It has turned into a loved image for New Zealanders, lovingly known as Kiwis. This epithet mirrors the native untamed life as well as exemplifies a feeling of public pride and character. The kiwi's relationship with the nation is commended in different structures, from public images and logos to casual articulations and comprehensive developments. The Kiwi, with its charming qualities and inborn connection to New Zealand, fills in as a binding together image that reverberates across different parts of the country's shared perspective.

The foundations of the epithet "Place that is known for the Kiwi" venture profound into New Zealand's rich social legacy, with the native Maori individuals assuming a focal part in molding the story. The Maori, who showed up in New Zealand around a long time back, carried with them a significant association with the land and a profound regard for the normal world. In Maori culture, the kiwi holds otherworldly importance, representing the association between individuals and the climate.

The Maori perspective, communicated through their practices, carvings, and stories, underscores the harmonious connection among humankind and nature. The kiwi, as a local animal varieties remarkably adjusted to the New Zealand climate, epitomizes this association. Customary Maori carvings, known as Whakairo, frequently portray the kiwi close by different images addressing familial stories and otherworldly convictions. The bird's presence in Maori craftsmanship and folklore highlights its social significance as a watchman of the land and an image of solidarity between past, present, and people in the future.

Notwithstanding its social imagery, the kiwi additionally holds monetary significance for New Zealand. The bird's picture is much of the time used in the travel industry advancements, marking, and showcasing materials, adding to the country's character on the worldwide stage. The Kiwi, with its beguiling and particular appearance, turns into a magnetic diplomat welcoming the world to investigate the marvels of the "Place that is known for the Kiwi."

The meaning of the kiwi goes past its portrayal in social and monetary circles; it is profoundly laced with New Zealand's obligation to preservation and ecological stewardship. As a flightless bird powerless against presented hunters, the kiwi populace confronted critical difficulties, prompting a decrease in numbers. Perceiving the direness of safeguarding this notable species, New Zealand set out on aggressive preservation drives pointed toward protecting the kiwi and its regular living space.

Various untamed life safe-havens and preservation projects have been laid out all through the nation, committed to the insurance and recovery of the kiwi populace. These drives include hunter control measures, living space rebuilding, and local area commitment to guarantee the endurance of this interesting bird. The Branch of Protection (DOC), an administration office, assumes a vital part in planning these endeavors, working in a joint effort with neighborhood networks, confidential associations, and worldwide accomplices.

One of the most eminent drives is Activity Savings, a preservation program that includes eliminating kiwi eggs from the wild, bring forth them in controlled conditions, and raising the chicks until they are sufficiently huge to protect themselves against hunters. When the youthful kiwis arrive at a specific size and weight, they are delivered once more into their regular living space, adding to the revival of wild populaces. These preservation attempts not just feature New Zealand's devotion to protecting its biodiversity yet in addition feature the personal association between individuals, the kiwi, and the land.

The moniker "Place that is known for the Kiwi" embodies the diverse relationship New Zealanders have with their current circumstance — a relationship established in social legacy, financial undertakings, and protection morals. It fills in as an update that the extraordinary personality of a country is complicatedly woven into the texture of its regular miracles and the endeavors made to safeguard them. The kiwi, as an image, epitomizes the soul of strength, transformation, and the aggregate liability of individuals to shield the valuable biodiversity that characterizes the "Place where there is the Kiwi."

The epithet "Place that is known for the Kiwi" is an idyllic articulation that exemplifies the profundity and lavishness of New Zealand's personality. It fills in as a scaffold between the native Maori culture, the country's special biodiversity, and its obligation to protection. The kiwi, with its charming qualities and social imagery, remains as a living demonstration of the interconnectedness of individuals and the climate. As New Zealand keeps on exploring the difficulties of the cutting edge world, the kiwi stays an image of strength, solidarity, and the persevering through soul of the "Place that is known for the Kiwi."

1.2 Explore the symbolism of the kiwi bird and its representation of New Zealand's natural wonders.

The kiwi bird, with its charming appearance and unmistakable qualities, remains as a strong image of New Zealand's regular miracles, exemplifying the country's special personality and its profound association with the climate. As we dig into the imagery of the kiwi, we unwind a story that entwines social importance, environmental strength, and the continuous protection endeavors that highlight the significance of safeguarding this famous species.

At the core of the kiwi's imagery lies its status as a quintessentially New Zealand animal. As a flightless, nighttime bird endemic to the islands, the kiwi is an image of the country's segregation and unmistakable biodiversity. Its presence in the wild is a sign of the country's obligation to protecting its normal legacy and the flexibility of its biological systems. The kiwi, through its variation to the New Zealand climate, has turned into a living image that embodies the quintessence of the land.

In Maori culture, the kiwi holds otherworldly importance and assumes a part in the rich embroidery of fantasies and legends. The Maori, the native individuals of New Zealand, showed up on these shores a while back, carrying with them a profound veneration for the normal world. In Maori folklore, birds, including the kiwi, are many times thought about couriers, overcoming any barrier between the natural domain and the profound space. The kiwi's special qualities, like its nighttime propensities and particular appearance, make it an animal of secret and interest in Maori stories.

In customary Maori carvings, known as Whakairo, the kiwi is many times portrayed close by different images addressing tribal stories, ancestry, and associations with the land. These carvings, unpredictably created and wealthy in imagery, act as a visual language that imparts the profound qualities and social character of the Maori public. The kiwi, with its job as a gatekeeper of the land, turns into a strong similitude for the reliance among mankind and nature, mirroring the Maori perspective that stresses concordance and equilibrium.

The kiwi's social importance reaches out past folklore and workmanship to turn into a necessary piece of contemporary New Zealand personality. New Zealanders, casually known as Kiwis, have taken on the bird as an image of public pride. The Kiwi fills in as a binding together seal that rises above social and ethnic limits, typifying a common association with the land. This association is reflected in ordinary language, where the expression "Kiwi" is utilized not exclusively to allude to the bird yet additionally as a conversational moniker for individuals of New Zealand.

The kiwi's representative significance is additionally enhanced by its job in forming the nation's monetary and the travel industry character. The bird's picture is unmistakably highlighted in public images, logos, and advertising materials, both locally and universally. The Kiwi, with its enchanting and particular appearance, turns into a charming envoy welcoming the world to investigate the miracles of the "Place where there is the Kiwi." It represents something other than a types of bird; it addresses a whole country's ethos, its relationship with the climate, and the qualities that characterize its kin.

Past its social imagery, the kiwi holds environmental importance as a cornerstone animal types in New Zealand's biological systems. As a flightless bird with restricted guards, the kiwi is especially helpless against presented hunters, like rodents, stoats, and possums, which were acquainted with the islands by European pioneers.

The decrease in kiwi populaces because of predation turned into a preservation concern, provoking deliberate endeavors to secure and restore the species.

Preservation drives pointed toward shielding the kiwi have turned into a basic part of New Zealand's obligation to ecological stewardship. The Division of Protection (DOC), an administration organization, assumes an essential part in planning and carrying out preservation techniques to guarantee the endurance of the kiwi and other jeopardized species. The earnestness of these endeavors is highlighted by the way that few kiwi species are named either imperiled or defenseless.

One of the most outstanding preservation programs is Activity Savings, which includes the expulsion of kiwi eggs from the wild, bring forth them in controlled conditions, and raising the chicks until they are adequately huge to protect themselves against hunters. When the youthful kiwis arrive at a specific size and weight, they are once again introduced into their regular territories, adding to the revival of wild populaces. These drives show the profundity of New Zealand's obligation to protecting its one of a kind biodiversity and guaranteeing that people in the future can encounter the regular miracles represented by the kiwi.

The kiwi's importance as a protection symbol isn't restricted to its own species; it stretches out to more extensive environmental endeavors. The conservation of the kiwi and its living space adds to the assurance of whole biological systems, cultivating the wellbeing and equilibrium of New Zealand's common habitat. The preservation story encompassing the kiwi fills in as a mobilizing point for local area commitment, training, and worldwide cooperation, underlining the interconnectedness of worldwide endeavors to safeguard imperiled species and save biodiversity.

As an image of biological flexibility, the kiwi mirrors the continuous exchange among humankind and the climate. Its story exemplifies the difficulties presented by presented species, natural surroundings misfortune, and the more extensive issues of environmental change. The preservation drives based on the kiwi act as an encouraging sign, delineating how aggregate endeavors can have a substantial effect in protecting the normal ponders that characterize the "Place that is known for the Kiwi."

The kiwi's imagery additionally stretches out into the domain of natural schooling and mindfulness. Instructive projects, interpretive focuses, and drives pointed toward encouraging a feeling of natural obligation use the kiwi as a point of convergence. By interfacing individuals with the kiwi's story, these drives motivate a more profound appreciation for the interconnected snare of life and the significance of individual and aggregate activities in safeguarding the planet's biodiversity.

The imagery of the kiwi bird is a multi-layered story that winds around together social importance, biological significance, and protection tries. As a social symbol, the kiwi addresses the profound association between the Maori public and the land, typifying a feeling of solidarity and equilibrium. As a public image, the Kiwi mirrors the pride and character of New Zealanders, rising above social and ethnic limits. Biologically, the kiwi fills in as a cornerstone animal groups, provoking protection endeavors that stretch out past the safeguarding of a solitary animal groups to the security of whole environments.

The tale of the kiwi is a demonstration of the multifaceted connection among mankind and the climate, featuring the difficulties presented by natural corruption and the flexibility expected to beat them. The continuous protection endeavors encompassing the kiwi show New Zealand's obligation to ecological stewardship and the getting through soul of the "Place that is known for the Kiwi." As the kiwi keeps on representing the interconnectedness of social character, environmental wellbeing, and preservation morals, it welcomes individuals all over the planet to participate in the aggregate liability of saving the normal ponders that characterize this novel and charming area.

1.3 Brief overview of the diverse landscapes and cultures in Aotearoa.

Aotearoa, usually known as New Zealand, unfurls as an embroidery of different scenes and societies that enrapture the creative mind of the people who investigate its islands. The geological extravagance of this Pacific country, settled in the southwestern piece of the sea, is reflected by the social variety that stems from its native Maori roots and the impacts of ensuing floods of pioneers. This short outline plans to typify the quintessence of Aotearoa by digging into its fluctuated landscapes, from snow-covered mountains to sandy sea shores, and by investigating the remarkable mix of Maori and European societies that characterize the country's personality.

The dazzling scenes of Aotearoa act as a demonstration of the country's land variety, where each go of the street uncovers another feature of normal magnificence. The South Island, described by its glorious Southern Alps, presents a rough territory decorated with ice sheets, high knolls, and mirror-like lakes. Aoraki/Mount Cook, the country's most elevated top, punctures the sky, directing a scene that exemplifies the crude power and quality of nature. The Fiordland Public Park, settled in the southwestern corner, uncovers a sensational fjord scene, with flowing cascades, sheer precipices, and tranquil coves like Milford Sound, welcoming voyagers to observe the dazzling greatness of the South Island.

Differentiating the South, the North Island unfurls with its geothermal miracles and lavish scenes. Rotorua, arranged in the Taupo Volcanic Zone, grandstands the World's geothermal powers with percolating mud pools, steaming fountains, and beautiful natural aquifers.

The Tongariro Public Park, an UNESCO World Legacy Site, flaunts dynamic volcanoes and emerald lakes, offering a striking difference to the serene magnificence tracked down somewhere else on the island. Brilliant sea shores stretch along the North Island's coast, welcoming sun-searchers to loll in the glow of the Pacific sun and investigate the marine ponders that possess its waters.

The shore of Aotearoa, bordered with sandy sea shores and tough precipices, gives a jungle gym to open air devotees. Abel Tasman Public Park, situated at the highest point of the South Island, is eminent for its brilliant sea shores, turquoise waters, and waterfront climbing trails. The Coromandel Promontory, on the North Island, is decorated with separated inlets, boiling water sea shores, and lavish rainforests, offering a beautiful departure for those looking for serenity in the midst of nature's marvels. As waves run into the coastlines and the pungent breeze swirls around, the beach front scenes of Aotearoa allure explorers to drench themselves in the excellence of the Pacific.

However, past the charm of its normal scenes, Aotearoa's social lavishness is similarly enthralling. The Maori, the native individuals of New Zealand, have a significant association with the land, and their social legacy pervades each feature of Aotearoa's personality. The haka, a conventional Maori war dance, is maybe one of the most famous articulations of Maori culture, a strong presentation that conveys strength, solidarity, and regard. Carvings, or Whakairo, enhance meeting houses and consecrated spaces, portraying tribal stories and profound associations with the land. The unpredictable examples and imagery inside these carvings act as a visual language, recounting the tales of the Maori public and their persevering through relationship with Aotearoa.

The idea of mana, a Maori expression indicating otherworldly power and authority, highlights the regard and worship the Maori have for their normal environmental elements. Mountains, waterways, and woodlands are not simply actual substances but rather epitomize profound importance, becoming storehouses of stories, customs, and hereditary associations. The interconnectedness of the Maori with the land is apparent in their comprehensive perspective, where the prosperity of the climate and the prosperity of individuals are entwined.

As Aotearoa's social account unfurls, the European impact, prevalently from English pioneers, meshes into the texture of the country. The impact of Maori and European societies has formed a remarkable personality described by the concurrence and incorporation of different customs. European engineering stands one next to the other with conventional Maori meeting houses, and English and Maori language coincide, mirroring a promise to regarding both social legacies. The mixing of these impacts is clear in human expression, food, and day to day existence of Aotearoa, making an energetic and comprehensive social scene.

The Deal of Waitangi, endorsed in 1840 between the English Crown and Maori bosses, assumes a urgent part in molding the connection between the two societies. While expected to lay out an organization and safeguard the privileges of the Maori, the understanding and execution of the settlement have been dependent upon verifiable intricacies. Endeavors to address verifiable complaints and advance compromise have been progressing, with the Waitangi Council giving a stage to the goal of issues connected with the settlement.

Contemporary New Zealand is an impression of this continuous exchange between societies, a powerful interchange that adds to the country's personality. The acknowledgment of Te Reo Maori, the Maori language, as an authority language of Aotearoa represents a pledge to saving and reviving Maori culture. Social celebrations, expressions occasions, and the festival of Matariki, the Maori New Year, further add to the energy of Aotearoa's social scene.

In the domain of expressions and writing, Aotearoa flaunts a rich and different embroidery of imaginative articulation. From the persuasive composition of creators like Katherine Mansfield and Janet Edge to the visual specialties of contemporary Maori craftsmen, the imaginative soul of Aotearoa mirrors the country's social profundity and variety. The actual scene frequently fills in as a material for imaginative undertakings, moving painters, scholars, and producers to catch the embodiment of the islands in their work.

Aotearoa's obligation to ecological maintainability is reflected in its preservation endeavors and drives to safeguard its remarkable biodiversity. The Division of Protection (DOC) assumes a significant part in overseeing public parks, stores, and natural life safe-havens, guaranteeing the conservation of endemic species and the rebuilding of environments. Preservation projects, like the expulsion of presented hunters from specific islands, add to the security of local greenery, exemplifying Aotearoa's devotion to ecological stewardship.

Aotearoa unfurls as a domain of unmatched magnificence, where different scenes and societies meet to make a novel and charming objective. From the snow-covered pinnacles of the Southern Alps to the brilliant sea shores of the Coromandel, the islands of New Zealand offer an excursion through a horde of regular miracles. The Maori social legacy, well established in the land and communicated through haka, carvings, and a significant association with nature, adds a layer of profound importance to the scenes.

At the same time, the coordination of European impacts, formed by the Settlement of Waitangi and continuous social discourse, makes a social scene that is dynamic, comprehensive, and intelligent of Aotearoa's personality. The obligation to ecological supportability, apparent in preservation drives and the acknowledgment of the characteristic worth of the land, highlights the country's commitment to saving its normal marvels for a long time into the future. Aotearoa remains as a demonstration of the amicable conjunction of different scenes and societies, welcoming voyagers to investigate the diverse magnificence that characterizes the core of the Pacific.

CHAPTER 2

"Nature's Canvas"

Nature's Material spreads out before our eyes, a steadily changing magnum opus that winds around together the energetic embroidery of the normal world. It is a structure of scenes and biological systems, a display where each stroke of variety, each shape of land, and the tune of stirring leaves recount an account of the World's getting through excellence. From magnificent mountains to tranquil knolls, thick woods to undulating streams, Nature's Material is a demonstration of the planet's creative ability.

High in the Andean pinnacles, the material starts with the snow-covered grandness of transcending mountains. The rough magnificence of pinnacles like the Aconcagua in South America or the Himalayas in Asia catches the creative mind, their culminations puncturing the sky. These huge models of rock and ice stand as sentinels, their inclines painted with the shades of high verdure that grip industriously to the meager air. The uneven scenes, molded by geographical powers over ages, inspire a feeling of wonderment and modesty, welcoming us to examine the World's considerable power and flexibility.

As the material plunges from elevated levels, it advances into the undulating slopes and valleys that describe immense scenes. Moving knolls, spotted with wildflowers that influence in the delicate breeze, make a peaceful orchestra of varieties. The juxtaposition of light and shadow on the undulating landscape projects a steadily moving example, a play of nature's chiaroscuro. Whether it's the Scottish High countries, the Tuscan open country, or the broad grasslands of the American Midwest, these scenes summon a feeling of immortality, welcoming us to interface with the rhythms of the Earth.

The material stretches out its compass to embrace the verdant hug of thick woodlands, where the murmuring leaves structure a shelter above. From the transcending redwoods of California to the supernatural mild rainforests of the Pacific Northwest, the variety of vegetation makes a rich mosaic. Each tree, a sentinel of time, demonstrates the veracity of hundreds of years of development, seasons, and the recurring pattern of life. The woodland floor, covered with fallen leaves and dappled daylight, turns into a phase for the sensitive dance of organisms and the complicated communications among greenery.

Streams, similar to fluid brushstrokes, cut their direction through Nature's Material, molding scenes and supporting life along their courses. The crooked bends of the Amazon, the lofty progression of the Nile, and the perfect magnificence of the New Zealand streams add to the multifaceted examples that effortlessness the material. These streams act as helps, supporting biological systems, giving food, and mirroring the encompassing scenes like gleaming mirrors. The cadenced progression of waterways turns into an illustration for the interconnectedness of every single living thing, an indication of the fragile equilibrium that supports the planet.

Nature's Material stretches out its range to the huge territories of deserts, where the World's tones are refined to their most basic structures. The moving sands of the Sahara, the extraordinary scenes of the Atacama, and the dream-like excellence of the Australian Outback feature the unmistakable difference among light and shadow. Notwithstanding the brutal circumstances, life perseveres in the desert, adjusted to the limits of temperature and aridity. The strength of desert greenery turns into a demonstration of nature's capacity to flourish in even the most difficult conditions.

The material unfurls underneath the sea's surface, where an outsider universe of miracles anticipates investigation. Coral reefs, with their kaleidoscope of varieties and perplexing designs, look like a submerged city abounding with life. The profound void, strange and unknown, is home to odd animals adjusted to the devastating strain and never-ending haziness. The sea's flows, as brushstrokes moving, make a dance of marine life, from smooth ocean turtles to grand whales. The marine domain, an imperative part of Nature's Material, addresses both the support of life and an environment of sensitive equilibrium.

The skies above complete Nature's Material with the steadily changing display of mists, the dance of daylight and twilight, and the amazing scene of heavenly bodies. From the sensational shades of dawn over the African savannah to the ethereal sparkle of Aurora Borealis in the Cold Circle, the sky turns into a powerful background that shapes the temperament and mood of the normal world. Birds in flight, their wings slicing through the air like strokes of calligraphy, add to the ethereal verse that graces the material.

Nature's Material isn't just a visual display yet an ensemble of sounds that reverberate across its immense span. The melodic trilling of crickets in a glade, the musical crashing of waves on a shore, the eerie call of a far off wolf in the timberland — this large number of hear-able components add to the vivid experience of the normal world. The breeze stirring through leaves, the delicate chatter of a stream, and the agreeable chorale of a rainforest act as nature's own creations, welcoming us to tune in and become receptive to the ensemble of life.

Inside the perplexing subtleties of Nature's Material, there lies a significant interconnectedness. Each component, from the littlest microorganisms to the most terrific geographical developments, assumes a part in a huge, perplexing trap of life. The sensitive dance of fertilization, the hunter prey connections in the collective of animals, and the harmonious associations between species all add to the strength and maintainability of biological systems. Nature's Material is a demonstration of the sensitive equilibrium that supports life on The planet, an equilibrium that is progressively weak notwithstanding human effect.

As stewards of Nature's Material, humankind holds both the paintbrush and the obligation to save its trustworthiness. The material, a wellspring of motivation and comfort, entices us to see the value in its magnificence and figure out the significant effect of our activities. Preservation endeavors, reasonable practices, and an aggregate obligation to ecological stewardship are fundamental brushes in the possession of the people who try to safeguard and save the magnum opus that is Nature's Material.

In the Anthropocene time, the material bears the hints of human impact, from deforestation and contamination to environmental change. The once-unblemished scenes presently convey the signs of our presence, and the fragile biological systems are confronting remarkable difficulties. However, in the midst of the worries, there is trust — the expectation that by perceiving our job as overseers of Nature's Material, we can work aggregately to reestablish and safeguard the multifaceted magnificence that characterizes our planet.

The enthusiasm for Nature's Material isn't only a tasteful pursuit; it is an affirmation of our interconnectedness with the Earth. The soundness of the planet straightforwardly impacts our prosperity, and the protection of biodiversity is critical for the endurance of innumerable species, including our own. Nature's Material, with its horde tones and structures, turns into a mirror mirroring the fragile equilibrium of life — an equilibrium that requires our regard, understanding, and purposeful endeavors to sustain and safeguard it for a long time into the future.

2.1 Dive into the breathtaking landscapes, from the lush greenery of Fiordland to the snow-capped peaks of the Southern Alps.

Leaving on an excursion through the captivating scenes of New Zealand is much the same as venturing into a strange dreamscape, where each go uncovers a stunning show-stopper created essentially's hands. The verdant charm of Fiordland, with its rich vegetation and emotional fjords, stands out wonderfully from the transcending magnificence of the Southern Alps, delegated with sparkling snow. This odyssey through New Zealand's different geology is a demonstration of the country's status as a visual ensemble of scenes, each note fitting with the close to make an unrivaled crescendo of regular magnificence.

Fiordland, settled in the southwestern corner of the South Island, arises as an emerald gem in New Zealand's crown. The inlets, cut by old icy masses, weave their direction through transcending bluffs, making a scene that is both glorious and ethereal. Milford Sound, maybe the most famous of these fjords, is a visual spectacle of sheer stone countenances, flowing cascades, and mirror-like waters that mirror the encompassing pinnacles. The glory of Milford Sound is uplifted via milestones, for example, Miter Pinnacle, which penetrates the sky, and Bowen Falls, a smooth strip of water that slips from the levels above.

As one submerges into Fiordland's lavish vegetation, a feeling of serenity wraps the spirit. Thick rainforests shroud the lofty slants, their foliage abounding with life. Old trees, hung in greenery and plants, stand as quiet sentinels, demonstrating the veracity of the progression of time. The air is loaded up with the tune of birdsong, reverberating through the verdant overhangs. Local species, for example, the notable Kiwi bird find shelter in this immaculate climate, their reality entwined with the perplexing trap of life that flourishes in Fiordland's biodiversity.

The wizardry of Fiordland stretches out underneath the surface, where the inlets' waters have a flourishing marine environment. Dolphins energetically dance in the bow rushes of boats, and fur seals loll on rough outcrops. Underneath the surface, interesting dark coral woods and energetic ocean anemones make a kaleidoscope of varieties. The interconnectedness of Fiordland's earthly and marine environments highlights its status as a safe-haven for biodiversity, a living demonstration of the fragile equilibrium that supports the district's normal marvels.

Leaving the lavish hug of Fiordland, the excursion takes an emotional turn towards the Southern Alps, a mountain range that stretches like a spine across the South Island. These magnificent pinnacles, clad in snow for a huge piece of the year, offer a distinct difference to the verdant scenes of the coves. The Southern Alps, home to New Zealand's most noteworthy pinnacles, including Aoraki/Mount Cook, welcome globe-trotters and nature devotees to investigate their snow capped ponders.

Aoraki/Mount Cook, remaining at a rise of 3,724 meters (12,218 feet), is a telling presence on the Southern Alps' horizon. The mountain, named after the Maori expression for "cloud piercer," is a guide for mountain dwellers and an image of New Zealand's elevated greatness. The encompassing Aoraki/Mount Cook Public Park, an UNESCO World Legacy Site, includes icy masses, frigid lakes, and high knolls. Mueller Cottage, roosted on the Sealy Reach, offers all encompassing perspectives on Aoraki and the encompassing pinnacles, welcoming gutsy explorers to observe the exhibition of the Southern Alps.

The appeal of the Southern Alps stretches out past Aoraki/Mount Cook, with other unmistakable pinnacles, for example, Mount Trying and Mount Tasman adding to the reach's rough magnificence. Icy valleys, cut over centuries, make a scene of significant greatness, while elevated pools reflect the encompassing pinnacles like perfectly clear gems. The Tasman Icy mass, New Zealand's longest ice sheet, further upgrades the snow capped display, its ice develop-ments and precipices adding a unique component to the view.

The Southern Alps become a jungle gym for experience fans, offering a horde of exercises that praise the snow capped climate. Climbing trails wind through high glades, giving chances to observe the quality of endemic greenery, for example, the Mount Cook Lily. Mountain climbers, drawn by the test of over-coming transcending tops, test their courage on ice and rock. In winter, the Southern Alps change into a snow-shrouded wonderland, welcoming skiers and snowboarders to cut finds flawless slants. The unique idea of the Southern Alps guarantees that each season grants its own personality to the scene, from the energetic sprouts of spring to the ethereal quietness of a snow-covered winter.

As one explores the change from Fiordland toward the Southern Alps, the different scenes of New Zealand become a living demonstration of the country's land history. The impact of structural plates, the chiseling powers of icy masses, and the interminable dance of normal components have fashioned a scene that is however unique as it seems to be stunning. The Southern Alps, with their snow capped quality, stand as a demonstration of the World's groundbreaking power, while Fiordland, with its fjords and rainforests, bears the signs of old chilly movement. This geographical embroidery paints an account of flexibility, variation, and the consistently developing nature of the New Zealand scene.

The convergence of these two differentiating scenes — the rich plant life of Fiordland and the snow-covered pinnacles of the Southern Alps — additionally reflects the crossing point of social accounts in New Zealand. The Maori, with their profound association with the land, weave stories and legends that mirror the stunning excellence of these normal miracles. The Southern Alps, frequently alluded to as "Ka Tiritiri o te Moana" in Maori, signifying "The Pinnacles of the Sea," hold profound importance as a spot where heavenly and natural domains meet.

Likewise, Fiordland's fjords, with their precarious bluffs and intelligent waters, are in many cases considered by the Maori as crafted by a pussyfooting divinity who cut the scene with accuracy. The mix of Maori folklore and other-worldliness with the regular habitat adds layers of social profundity to the generally significant scenes. The Maori idea of kaitiakitanga, or guardianship, underlines the obligation of people to really focus on and safeguard the land, perceiving the interconnectedness among individuals and the regular world.

New Zealand's scenes, with their dazzling excellence, have likewise assumed a huge part in the country's social character. The amazing view has filled in as the setting for various movies, generally quite the "Master of the Rings" and "The Hobbit" sets of three, where the country's different scenes turned into the artistic scenes of Center earth. The worldwide acknowledgment of New Zealand as a place that is known for unmatched excellence has supported the travel industry as well as added to the country's social product, imparting the wizardry of its scenes to crowds all over the planet.

The juxtaposition of Fiordland and the Southern Alps additionally features New Zealand's obligation to natural preservation and maintainability. The two districts are safeguarded by public parks and UNESCO World Legacy Destinations, guaranteeing that their interesting environments and social qualities are saved for people in the future. The Branch of Preservation (DOC), New Zealand's administration organization devoted to preservation, assumes an essential part in dealing with these safeguarded regions, carrying out protection drives, and cultivating local area commitment to guarantee the continuous wellbeing of these scenes.

In Fiordland, where the sensitive equilibrium of environments is especially helpless, preservation endeavors center around bug control to safeguard local greenery. The presentation of obtrusive species represents a huge danger to New Zealand's biodiversity, and drives like the evacuation of acquainted hunters contribute with the protection of the country's novel biological systems. The Southern Alps, with their elevated knolls and delicate conditions, additionally benefit from protection programs pointed toward moderating the effect of human exercises and environmental change.

As New Zealand keeps on exploring the sensitive convergence of natural protection, social legacy, and the travel industry, the scenes of Fiordland and the Southern Alps stay integral to the country's character. The capable delight and stewardship of these regular miracles are fundamental for the conservation of the very quintessence that makes New Zealand a safe-haven of unmatched magnificence.

2.2 Explore the geothermal wonders of Rotorua and the volcanic landscapes that shape the North Island.

The North Island of New Zealand, a place that is known for geothermal wonders and volcanic scenes, unfurls a charming story composed by the World's red hot powers.

Among the heap ponders that effortlessness this district, Rotorua remains as a throbbing heart, a geothermal center where the World's interior energy makes its presence felt in sensational style. From bubbling mud pools to emitting fountains, the geothermal marvels of Rotorua give a hypnotizing look into the unique powers that shape New Zealand's North Island.

Arranged inside the Taupo Volcanic Zone, Rotorua is a topographical area of interest described by serious volcanic action. The city and its environmental factors brag a supernatural scene molded by geothermal elements that have enthralled the creative mind for quite a long time. The rich Maori social legacy further interweaves with the geothermal scenes, as the native individuals perceive and venerate the profound meaning of these hearty peculiarities.

Te Puia, a geothermal save and social focus in Rotorua, offers a passage into the entrancing universe of geothermal miracles. As guests step onto the grounds of Te Puia, the earth underneath their feet appears to murmur with energy. Pohutu, one of the Southern Half of the globe's biggest dynamic fountains, remains as a characteristic wonder, delivering tufts of steam and water up high at ordinary stretches. The musical dance of Pohutu turns into a visual orchestra, a sign of the geothermal powers that heartbeat underneath the World's surface.

Around Pohutu, the scene is spotted with fumaroles, underground aquifers, and bubbling mud pools. These geothermal elements, each with its extraordinary qualities, make a strange scene that brings out both miracle and regard. The Champagne Pool, a dynamic underground aquifer with shades of orange and turquoise, mirrors the mineral-rich waters that air pocket up from the World's profundities. The percolating mud pools, known as Ngāraratuatara, paint the ground with their grayish tones, making a scene suggestive of a no nonsense work of art.

As the geothermal miracles of Rotorua allure investigation, the social account of the Maori public unfurls couple. The Maori, the native individuals of New Zealand, have possessed this geothermally dynamic district for a really long time. For their purposes, the geothermal elements are normal peculiarities as well as appearances of the World's life force, or mauri. The association between the Maori and the land is profoundly otherworldly, and the geothermal scenes hold a consecrated importance in their social practices.

Te Puia, as well as being a geothermal hold, fills in as a social place where guests can draw in with Maori customs. The Whakarewarewa Town, situated inside Te Puia, is a living Maori people group that has adjusted to coincide with the geothermal climate. Conventional Maori engineering, including unpredictably cut gathering houses, or wharenui, remains in the midst of the geothermal highlights, offering a visual portrayal of the amicable connection between the Maori and their environmental elements.

The Pohutu Social Venue at Te Puia gives a stage to the sharing of Maori performing expressions, including the haka — a strong dance that conveys strength, solidarity, and regard.

The reverberation of social customs inside the geothermal scenes of Rotorua makes a comprehensive encounter, where guests witness the World's crude power as well as submerge themselves in the residing embroidery of Maori legacy.

Past Rotorua, the whole North Island bears the characteristics of volcanic action, displaying a scene etched by both old and contemporary emissions. The story of volcanic scenes unfurls in the remainders of calderas, cavities, and magma streams that shape the landscape. One of the most notorious volcanic elements is Mount Tarawera, a stratovolcano situated toward the southeast of Rotorua. In 1886, Mount Tarawera emitted in a disastrous occasion that decisively changed the scene and guaranteed lives, abandoning the Waimangu Volcanic Valley — a demonstration of the crude force of volcanic powers.

Waimangu, the most youthful geothermal framework on the planet, is a residing research center where the World's regenerative power is in plain view. The valley features the perplexing interchange between geothermal action and natural restoration. Skillet Lake, the world's biggest underground aquifer by volume, mirrors the changing shades of the mineral-rich waters. Hellfire Pit, with its surging steam and lively shades, is an indication of the underground powers that keep on molding the land.

The Tongariro Public Park, an UNESCO World Legacy Site, is one more section in the story of the North Island's volcanic heritage. Overwhelmed by three dynamic volcanoes — Mount Ruapehu, Mount Ngauruhoe, and Mount Tongariro — the recreation area's scenes are a concentrate in contrasts. Elevated glades, frigid valleys, and flawless lakes coincide with the distinct excellence of volcanic holes and magma streams. The Tongariro Elevated Crossing, proclaimed as one of the world's greatest day climbs, takes travelers through this unique scene, offering all encompassing perspectives on the volcanic territory.

Mount Ruapehu, the most noteworthy top on the North Island, fills in as both a sporting jungle gym and a sign of the district's land power. Ski resorts enhance its slants in winter, while in summer, explorers and climbers rise its levels to observe the all encompassing vistas of the volcanic level. The Whakapapa Ski Field, settled on Mount Ruapehu, turns into a frigid material where lovers cut trails in the midst of the volcanic pinnacles.

As the North Island's volcanic scenes unfurl, so does the consciousness of the powerful geographical cycles that keep on forming the district. New Zealand's situation on the Pacific Ring of Fire, where structural plates impact and interface, guarantees that volcanic action stays a characterizing element of the scene. While the World's interior powers can appear in marvelous emissions, they additionally add to the formation of ripe soils, underground aquifers, and geothermal energy assets that benefit the district.

Rotorua, with its geothermal marvels, and the more extensive volcanic scenes of the North Island, welcome thought of the sensitive harmony between the World's horrendous and regenerative powers. The geothermal highlights, while exhibiting the crude energy underneath the surface, likewise act as tokens of the requirement for capable stewardship. In a world wrestling with the outcomes of environmental change and ecological debasement, the practical use of geothermal assets for energy turns into a point of convergence for development and protection.

New Zealand, with its obligation to natural maintainability, bridles geothermal energy as an inexhaustible asset. Geothermal power plants, decisively situated in regions with high geothermal movement, create power by taking advantage of the World's regular intensity. The use of geothermal energy lines up with New Zealand's objective to lessen its carbon impression and change towards cleaner, practical energy sources. The nation's spearheading endeavors in geothermal energy highlight an agreeable concurrence with the volcanic scenes that characterize its personality.

2.3 Highlight the significance of New Zealand's flora and fauna in shaping its natural beauty.

New Zealand, an archipelago settled in the southwestern Pacific Sea, flaunts an extraordinary and various exhibit of verdure that assumes a significant part in molding the country's normal excellence. The islands, segregated for a long period of time, have developed a particular environment set apart by endemic species, old woods, and a fragile natural equilibrium. From the notable silver greenery to the tricky kiwi bird, the meaning of New Zealand's plant and creature life stretches out past simple style, encapsulating the country's biological wealth, social legacy, and obligation to protection.

The greenery of New Zealand remains as a demonstration of the islands' segregation and the versatile development of plant species without any mammalian herbivores. Maybe the most significant of these is the silver greenery (Cyathea dealbata), a public image that decorates the nation's banner. The silver underside of its fronds, apparent in moonlight, brought about the Maori name "ponga," which is inseparable from immaculateness and excellence. The silver plant isn't only a herbal wonder however a social symbol, addressing the interconnectedness of nature and the Maori public.

Endemic plant species add to the richness of New Zealand's scenes, making vistas that are both spellbinding and particular. The kahikatea (Dacrycarpus dacrydioides), a transcending conifer, is one of the country's old fortunes, for certain trees going back more than a thousand years. These goliaths of the backwoods stand as gatekeepers, their presence adding to the feeling of agelessness that infests New Zealand's antiquated forests.

The Pohutukawa (Metrosideros excelsa), known as the New Zealand Christmas tree, adds an eruption of dark red to seaside scenes during the southern half of the globe's late spring. Its dynamic blossoms and capacity to flourish in testing beach front circumstances make it an image of strength and regular excellence. The Pohutukawa isn't only respected for its feel however is profoundly woven into the social texture, representing the appearance of summer and the soul of local meetings.

The local flax plant, or harakeke (Phormium tenax), holds social importance for the Maori, who have used its flexible strands for winding around and making for a really long time. The perplexing craft of flax winding around, known as raranga, produces a scope of customary things, including crates, mats, and dress. Harakeke isn't simply a utilitarian plant however a living association with Maori customs, epitomizing the profound regard and correspondence between the native individuals and the land.

New Zealand's woods, overwhelmed by local species like the strong kahikatea, rimu, and totara, add to the country's standing as one of the world's last shelters for old vegetation. The podocarp and beech woods, with their greenery covered trees and productive birdlife, make a captivating air that summons a feeling of ancient wild. These timberlands are not simply scenes to be respected yet safe-havens for biodiversity, lodging a variety of plant species, organisms, and lichens that by and large structure a perplexing trap of life.

In juxtaposition to the local greenery, New Zealand likewise wrestles with the effect of presented plant species, frequently alluded to as "weeds." Obtrusive plants, brought by human exercises, represent a danger to the local biological systems by outcompeting native verdure, modifying soil sythesis, and upsetting normal environments. Protection endeavors and drives by associations like the Branch of Protection (DOC) center around the annihilation of intrusive species, guaranteeing the conservation of New Zealand's exceptional organic legacy.

The meaning of New Zealand's fauna is similarly significant, with the islands being home to a scope of extraordinary and endemic species that have adjusted to the nation's separation. Among the most famous is the kiwi bird, a flightless, nighttime animal that has become inseparable from New Zealand's character. The kiwi's unmistakable appearance, with its long nose and brown, fluffy plumage, makes it a charming image of the country's regular legacy.

The kiwi holds social importance for the Maori, who look at it as a taonga, or treasure, and an image of their association with the land. The bird's name is gotten from the Maori language, and its presence in Maori folklore adds layers of imagery to its importance. Kiwi protection endeavors, including environment rebuilding and hunter control, highlight the obligation to guaranteeing the endurance of this remarkable and loved species.

Past the kiwi, New Zealand's avian variety incorporates the kea, a profoundly smart high parrot known for its energetic shenanigans and dynamic plumage. The kea's flexibility to the brutal elevated climate mirrors the strength of New Zealand's fauna, while its devilish way of behaving has charmed it to the two local people and guests. Preservation drives look to safeguard the kea and other local bird species from dangers like presented hunters and natural surroundings debasement.

The birdlife of New Zealand stretches out to seabird states, where species like the regal gooney bird and the little pixie tern track down safe-haven. The country's beach front conditions act as pivotal favorable places for these transitory birds, adding to the worldwide biodiversity of seabird populaces. The Otago Promontory, home to the world's just central area imperial gooney bird province, offers a brief look into the grand universe of these taking off seabirds.

Marine life further upgrades the biological woven artwork of New Zealand, with its encompassing seas abounding with assorted species. The fundamentally imperiled Maui's dolphin, one of the world's most uncommon dolphin species, possesses the beach front waters of the North Island. Preservation endeavors, including marine stores and defensive measures, expect to protect the territories of marine well evolved creatures and safeguard the strength of New Zealand's marine biological systems.

The meaning of New Zealand's widely varied vegetation is unpredictably attached to the idea of whakapapa, a Maori expression including parentage, heritage, and interconnectedness. Whakapapa reaches out past human heredity to incorporate the land, water, and every living being. The native perspective perceives the intrinsic worth of every species and their part in keeping up with the fragile equilibrium of environments.

Preservation drives in New Zealand are driven by the comprehension that the strength of environments is related with the prosperity of both vegetation. The Division of Preservation (DOC), laid out in 1987, assumes a focal part in overseeing and safeguarding the country's normal legacy. DOC's endeavors incorporate territory rebuilding, bother control programs, and the foundation of untamed life asylums to give places of refuge to imperiled species.

Hunter free drives, for example, the aggressive objective of making New Zealand hunter free by 2050, highlight the country's obligation to reestablishing and protecting its local environments. Presented mammalian hunters, including rodents, stoats, and possums, present critical dangers to local birdlife and plant species. Protectionists utilize imaginative methods, for example, the utilization of traps, lure stations, and hereditary advances, to alleviate the effect of these hunters on New Zealand's novel biodiversity.

The idea of kaitiakitanga, or guardianship, is profoundly imbued in Maori culture and reverberates with the more extensive ethos of natural stewardship in New Zealand.

The obligation to really focus on the land and its occupants stretches out to people, networks, and the public authority. Protection endeavors are co-operative undertakings that include organizations between native networks, researchers, policymakers, and the general population, mirroring a common obligation to defending New Zealand's normal legacy.

The meaning of New Zealand's greenery isn't restricted to environmental contemplations; it likewise reaches out to the country's social character and economy. The travel industry, a significant industry for New Zealand, is energized to a great extent by the charm of its novel scenes and the chance to observe the country's notorious untamed life. Guests are attracted to encounters, for example, whale watching in Kaikoura, birdwatching in local backwoods, and investigating marine stores, adding to the country's economy while cultivating an appreciation for its normal fortunes.

The entertainment world, with creations like "The Master of the Rings" and "The Hobbit" sets of three shot against the background of New Zealand's dazzling scenes, further intensifies the worldwide acknowledgment of the country's regular excellence. The depiction of New Zealand as a realistic heaven draws in vacationers as well as raises the country's profile as a worldwide forerunner in ecological preservation.

In spite of the steps in protection and the obligation to saving biodiversity, New Zealand faces continuous difficulties. Environmental change presents dangers to biological systems, influencing the conveyance and conduct of greenery. Expanded temperatures, changes in precipitation designs, and the escalation of outrageous climate occasions add to the weakness of local species. Versatile procedures, including territory rebuilding and environment strong preservation rehearses, are urgent for relieving the effect of environmental change on New Zealand's one of a kind biological systems.

The sensitive dance between human exercises and the regular world highlights the requirement for economical practices and an ethic of dependable conjunction. Farming, a fundamental piece of New Zealand's economy, has suggestions for land use, water quality, and biodiversity. Adjusting the requests of agribusiness with preservation goals requires creative methodologies, like regenerative cultivating rehearses and the assurance of riparian zones.

The meaning of New Zealand's widely varied vegetation in forming its regular magnificence stretches out a long ways past the tasteful allure of scenes and the charm of exceptional natural life. It encapsulates a complicated snare of biological connections, social customs, and a guarantee to ecological stewardship. From the antiquated kahikatea standing sentinel in local backwoods to the tricky kiwi bird exploring its nighttime environment, every species adds to the many-sided embroidered artwork of New Zealand's biodiversity.

The nation's widely varied vegetation are not uninvolved components but rather dynamic members in a powerful story of transformation, strength, and interconnectedness. The acknowledgment of the inherent worth of every species, combined with the Maori standards of whakapapa and kaitiakitanga, structures the groundwork of protection endeavors. New Zealand's obligation to being a gatekeeper of its normal legacy mirrors a more extensive worldwide basic to offset human exercises with the protection of the World's indispensable biodiversity.

As New Zealand proceeds with its excursion towards a more feasible and strong future, the meaning of its vegetation stays at the very front of public cognizance. The test isn't just to monitor what exists however to effectively take part in the recovery of environments, guaranteeing that people in the future acquire a land wealthy in biological variety and social dynamic quality. In the continuous story of New Zealand's normal magnificence, the vegetation are not simply detached characters; they are heroes in a story of conjunction, transformation, and the persevering through excellence of the islands' biological embroidery.

CHAPTER 3

"Blue Waters Beckon"

Blue waters, extending as may be obvious, summon a feeling of serenity and marvel. Whether lapping against brilliant shores, settled inside emotional fjords, or embracing coral reefs underneath the tropical sun, blue waters hold a certain charm that rises above topographical limits. This investigation into the domain of "Blue Waters Call" divulges the multi-layered magnificence, social importance, and natural significance of Earth's oceanic scenes.

The sea, with its tremendous span of dark blue tones, fills in as the planet's backbone, holding onto a stunning variety of life and impacting environment designs. The interconnectedness of Earth's seas assumes a pivotal part in supporting life in the world, controlling temperature, and creating a huge piece of the oxygen we relax. As the heartbeat of the Earth, the seas coax us to investigate their secrets and value the sensitive equilibrium that characterizes this indispensable biological system.

From the Cold to the Antarctic, the polar oceans display an exceptional appeal, delegated with spreads of drifting chunks of ice and intelligent sheets of ocean ice.

The Cold's ice-shrouded waters, outlined by shocking scenes of tundra and icy masses, have a sensitive dance of polar bears, seals, and transitory birds. These cold waters, frequently connected with the ethereal Aurora Borealis, cause to notice the effect of environmental change as increasing temperatures reshape the polar climate.

On the other hand, the Antarctic's frosty hug, encompassing the southernmost landmass, charms with its giant ice retires and transcending glacial masses. As a shelter for seals, penguins, and slippery marine life, the Antarctic waters offer a brief look into the flexibility of species adjusted to outrageous circumstances. The Antarctic, described by its perfect, immaculate excellence, fills in as a gauge for worldwide environment patterns and highlights the earnestness of saving Earth's polar locales.

Wandering into hotter scopes, the sky blue waters of tropical oceans become a jungle gym for dynamic coral reefs, overflowing with life. The Incomparable Boundary Reef, an UNESCO World Legacy Site, remains as a demonstration of the mind boggling biodiversity that flourishes underneath the surface. The vivid universe of coral developments, joined by a variety of marine species, coaxes jumpers and swimmers into a domain of unmatched magnificence. The delicate equilibrium of coral biological systems features the interconnectedness of marine life and the effect of human exercises on these sensitive submerged scenes.

The appeal of blue waters stretches out past the untamed sea to incorporate peaceful lakes and great fjords. New Zealand's Fiordland, with its profound, tight fjords embellished with intelligent waters, illustrates nature's glory. Milford Sound, settled inside Fiordland, enamors with flowing cascades, verdant bluffs, and a feeling of tranquility that rises above the substantial world. The juxtaposition of lavish plant life and the dark blue waters makes a visual orchestra, welcoming thought of the powers that shape these striking scenes.

Inland, lakes arise as gems in the scene, their blue waters reflecting the skies above. Lake Baikal, the world's most profound and most seasoned freshwater lake, supports Siberia in its cerulean hug. With endemic species, for example, the Baikal seal and an extraordinary biodiversity molded by its disengagement, Lake Baikal coaxes swashbucklers and researchers the same to investigate its profundities and unwind its environmental secrets. Blue waters, whether in sweeping seas or confined lakes, become materials that mirror the magnificence and variety of our planet.

Social accounts all over the planet entwine with blue waters, molding customs, livelihoods, and profound associations. The Mediterranean, a support of old civilizations, gives testimony regarding the recurring pattern of history against a scenery of sky blue oceans.

The interconnectedness of societies around the Mediterranean, from the Greeks and Romans to the Phoenicians, has been significantly affected by the abundance and difficulties introduced by these blue waters. Today, beach front networks keep on drawing food and motivation from the Mediterranean's hug.

In the Pacific, the immeasurability of the sea associates assorted island countries, each with its novel social character formed by the encompassing blue span. The Polynesians, ace pilots, investigated the Pacific's waters with heavenly route strategies, choosing distant islands and cultivating a profound association with the sea. The Pacific's blue waters, specked with coral atolls and volcanic islands, mirror the versatility and flexibility of the way of life that call these remote heavens home.

Blue waters are not only a background for human civilization; they are wellsprings of motivation, creative articulation, and otherworldly reflection. Specialists since the beginning of time have tried to catch the hypnotizing excellence of seas, lakes, and streams on material. From the seascapes of J.M.W. Turner to the oceanic works of art of Winslow Homer, the imaginative depiction of blue waters rises above the visual to summon feelings and a feeling of the magnificent.

The otherworldly meaning of blue waters is clear in strict customs around the world. The Ganges, a sacrosanct waterway in Hinduism, draws a huge number of pioneers who look for filtration and otherworldly restoration in its streaming waters. The custom of submerging oneself in the Ganges, known as Ganga snan, is a profoundly representative demonstration that rises above the actual domain, associating the person with the heavenly progression of life. The holiness of water reaches out past Hinduism, with streams, lakes, and seas holding otherworldly significance in assorted beliefs and social practices.

The interconnectedness of blue waters with human societies is likewise obvious in the sea customs that have molded civic establishments. Nautical social orders, from the Vikings to the Polynesians, have explored the seas, finding new terrains, laying out shipping lanes, and cultivating social trades. The sea Silk Street, an old organization of shipping lanes associating East and West, embodies the verifiable meaning of blue waters in working with worldwide business and social dissemination.

However, the captivating excellence and social meaning of blue waters face considerable difficulties in the 21st 100 years. Human exercises, including overfishing, contamination, and environmental change, present dangers to the soundness of marine biological systems and the fragile equilibrium of life underneath the waves. Coral fading, plastic contamination, and the fermentation of seas are distinct tokens of the critical requirement for preservation and supportable practices to safeguard Earth's blue waters.

Environmental change, driven by human-actuated ozone depleting substance outflows, enhances the dangers looked by seas and their biological systems. Rising ocean levels, outrageous climate occasions, and disturbances to marine food networks are among the outcomes of a warming planet. The criticalness to address environmental change lines up with the basic to protect the strength of blue waters and alleviate the effect on marine life and waterfront networks.

Preservation endeavors, driven by logical examination, global participation, and grassroots drives, mean to secure and reestablish the strength of blue waters. Marine safeguarded regions, intended to protect basic living spaces and biodiversity, add to the flexibility of sea environments. Drives to battle plastic contamination, advance practical fisheries, and diminish fossil fuel by-products highlight the aggregate liability to guarantee the life span of Earth's blue waters.

The Assembled Countries' Maintainable Advancement Objective 14, zeroed in on life beneath water, features the worldwide obligation to preserve and reasonably utilize the seas, oceans, and marine assets. The execution of measures to lessen overfishing, safeguard marine biodiversity, and address the effects of environmental change highlights the acknowledgment that the destiny of blue waters is interwoven with the prosperity of humankind.

3.1 Discover the pristine blue waters surrounding New Zealand, from the Tasman Sea to the Pacific Ocean.

New Zealand, an island country arranged in the southwestern Pacific Sea, is encircled by perfect blue waters that weave an embroidery of different marine conditions. From the rough shorelines of the Tasman Ocean to the turquoise scopes of the Pacific Sea, the encompassing waters of New Zealand coax with a remarkable mix of magnificence, biodiversity, and social importance.

The Tasman Ocean, named after the Dutch pioneer Abel Tasman, graces the western shores of New Zealand, isolating it from the mainland of Australia. The gathering point of the Tasman Ocean and the Southern Alps makes a sensational scene, where snow-covered tops outpouring down to meet the sea's edge. The West Shoreline of the South Island, rough and untamed, is a demonstration of the crude powers of nature that have formed New Zealand's western edges.

The Tasman Ocean, known for its dark blue waters, is a jungle gym for marine life that flourishes in the supplement rich flows. Seal states speck the rough shores, and seabirds dance on the updrafts, making a powerful scene of life against the setting of the ocean. The waterfront town of Kaikoura, settled between the Offshore Kaikoura Reach and the Pacific Sea, is prestigious for its marine biodiversity, offering a brief look into the lavishness of New Zealand's marine biological systems.

Kaikoura's submerged gorge, cut by old topographical cycles, make up-wellings of supplement rich waters. These supplement rich flows, ascending from the profundities of the Tasman Ocean, draw in an overflow of marine life, making Kaikoura a safe house for whales, dolphins, seals, and a bunch of fish animal types. The occupant sperm whales, with their notable accidents breaking the surface, are an image of the profound association between the earthly and marine domains in this waterfront heaven.

Whale watching visits in Kaikoura give a private experience these delicate monsters of the sea. Seeing a goliath sperm whale effortlessly exploring the waters, joined by the lively shenanigans of dim dolphins and the majestic presence of orcas, changes the Tasman Ocean into a living performance center of marine scene. The eco-the travel industry rehearses in Kaikoura stress the significance of capable connection with marine life, cultivating an agreeable connection among people and the regular world.

As we venture toward the east, the turquoise waters of the Pacific Sea embrace the eastern shores of New Zealand, offering a distinct difference to the wild magnificence of the Tasman Ocean. The Narrows of Bounty, appropriately named for its overflow of marine life, unfurls along the northeastern shore of the North Island. This waterfront district, with its sandy sea shores and purplish blue waters, epitomizes the unspoiled symbolism frequently connected with the Pacific Sea.

The Sound of Bounty isn't just a safe house for ocean side darlings yet in addition a safe-haven for marine biodiversity. The marine stores and beach front environments give asylum to a variety of species, from brilliant fish to complicated coral developments. The locale's coral reefs, however not quite so broad as those in heat and humidities, add to the rich mosaic of New Zealand's submerged scenes. Swimmers and jumpers investigating the waters of the Cove of Bounty experience an existence where kelp woods influence with the delicate flows, and schools of fish explore the complex territory.

Off the eastern bank of the North Island lies the famous White Island, a functioning stratovolcano that ascents magnificently from the ocean. Encircled by the sapphire waters of the Pacific, White Island is a land wonder and a demonstration of the unique powers that have formed New Zealand's islands. Directed visits to White Island permit guests to observe the steaming vents, dynamic sulfur stores, and the rough excellence of a functioning volcanic scene encompassed by perfect blue waters.

Further toward the north, the Unfortunate Knights Islands, a marine save and UNESCO World Legacy Site, coax with their emerald-green waters and lowered openings. The islands, named by Commander James Cook, are leftovers of old volcanic movement and presently abound with marine life. The submerged caverns and curves, shaped by the disintegrating powers of the ocean, make a dreamlike submerged domain where jumpers can investigate the dynamic biodiversity of subtropical waters.

The Hauraki Bay, encompassing the Auckland district, is an oceanic jungle gym where metropolitan life and regular magnificence meet. The bay is studded with islands, each with its interesting person and appeal. Waiheke Island, known for its grape plantations and imaginative networks, is embraced by the cerulean waters of the inlet. The juxtaposition of metropolitan Auckland against the background of the Hauraki Bay epitomizes the amicable concurrence of city life and the common habitat in New Zealand.

The marine stores inside the Hauraki Bay, like the Goat Island Marine Save, add to the preservation of marine biological systems and give a living lab to researchers and scientists. Goat Island, New Zealand's most memorable marine hold, permits guests to observe the regenerative force of marine conditions when safeguarded from fishing and other anthropogenic exercises. Swimmers in Goat Island's reasonable waters experience a submerged existence where kelp woods influence, and fish of different varieties and sizes explore the rough reefs.

New Zealand's southernmost city, Dunedin, ignores the South Pacific Sea, offering a brief look into the untamed excellence of the southern coast. The Otago Landmass, stretching out into the Pacific, is a shelter for seabirds, marine warm blooded creatures, and rough scenes. The Regal Gooney bird Center on Taiaroa Head gives an intriguing an open door to observe the grand gooney bird taking off over the untamed sea, embodying the opportunity and effortlessness related with the boundlessness of the Pacific.

As we navigate the blue waters that encompass New Zealand, the meaning of these marine conditions goes past their stylish allure. The seas assume a basic part in directing the planet's environment, impacting weather conditions, and giving a natural surroundings to a heap of animal categories. The interconnectedness of earthly and marine environments highlights the fragile equilibrium that supports life on The planet.

New Zealand's Maori culture, well established in the association among individuals and the regular world, mirrors the significance of blue waters in molding social personality. The waka, or conventional kayak, holds a focal spot in Maori imagery, addressing a method for route as well as the excursion of life. The sea, as a wellspring of food and a pathway for investigation, is imbued in Maori stories, melodies, and customs.

Customary fishing rehearses, went down through ages, accentuate the significance of manageability and regard for marine assets. The idea of kaitiakitanga, or guardianship, reaches out to the seas, featuring the obligation of people to secure and save the wellbeing of marine conditions. The social meaning of blue waters is additionally obvious in the conventional cutting of waka huia, or treasure boxes, embellished with marine themes that give proper respect to the sea's gifts.

The tradition of nautical and route, indispensable to Maori legacy, interlaces with the more extensive oceanic history of New Zealand. The appearance of European wayfarers and pioneers via ocean denoted a crucial part in the country's set of experiences. The blue waters that encompassed New Zealand became channels for social trade, exchange, and the foundation of seaside networks that would shape the nation's future.

In the contemporary setting, New Zealand's obligation to marine protection lines up with worldwide endeavors to address the difficulties confronting the world's seas. The foundation of marine safeguarded regions, maintainable fisheries the board, and drives to battle plastic contamination mirror a proactive way to deal with protecting the respectability of marine biological systems. The Blue Belt Program, a New Zealand-drove drive, looks to improve marine security in the country's elite monetary zone, highlighting the country's commitment to economical marine practices.

The effects of environmental change, appeared in rising ocean levels, sea fermentation, and changes in marine biodiversity, add direness to the requirement for worldwide coordinated effort in marine protection. New Zealand, as an individual from the Pacific people group, is keenly conscious about the weaknesses looked by island countries notwithstanding environment related difficulties. The Pacific Islands Discussion, a provincial association, gives a stage to discourse and participation on issues going from environmental change to marine asset the executives.

3.2 Explore the marine life, including whales, dolphins, and the unique yellow-eyed penguins.

The marine life encompassing New Zealand is an enrapturing and various display that unfurls across its immaculate blue waters. From the magnificent whales that explore the sea profundities to the fun loving dolphins moving on a superficial level and the idiosyncratic yellow-looked at penguins waddling along the shores, the rich embroidery of marine biodiversity in New Zealand is a demonstration of the environmental wealth and preservation endeavors that characterize the country.

Whales, among the biggest and most sensational animals on The planet, elegance the waters encompassing New Zealand. The country's extraordinary geological area, situated between the Tasman Ocean and the Pacific Sea, makes a transitory pathway for different whale species. The Kaikoura Gully, a submerged gorge off the shore of the South Island, assumes an essential part in drawing in whales to these supplement rich waters.

Kaikoura, famous as one of the most incredible spots for whale observing internationally, is a shelter for both occupant and transient whale species. The Sperm Whale, the biggest toothed whale and a notorious inhabitant of Kaikoura, is much of the time spotted cruising close to the surface. Seeing a sperm whale nimbly lifting its accident over the water prior to plummeting into the profundities is a mark snapshot of Kaikoura's whale-watching experience.

Notwithstanding sperm whales, other whale species, including humpback whales, pilot whales, and orcas, incessant the waters off Kaikoura. The orcas, known as the dominant hunters of the sea, display remarkable taking care of ways of behaving, like deliberate abandoning to get seals, making them a captivating subject of study for sea life researcher and an outright exhilarating sight for whale watchers.

The Southern Right Whale, recognized by the callosities on its head, is another species that graces New Zealand's waters, especially in the subantarctic locales. These delicate monsters were generally pursued really close to eradication, however preservation endeavors, including worldwide security arrangements, have added to the sluggish recuperation of Southern Right Whale populaces.

Dolphins, with their lively and social ways of behaving, are alluring occupants of New Zealand's seaside waters. The shadowy dolphin, portrayed by its unmistakable hourglass design on the flank, is a typical sight in the waters around the country. The Narrows of Islands, situated in the subtropical Northland locale, is a focal point for experiencing these gymnastic marine warm blooded creatures.

Dolphin-watching visits in the Cove of Islands give an open door to guests to observe the abundant presentations of gloomy dolphins as they jump, twist, and surf in the vessel's wake. The intuitive idea of these dolphins, frequently moving toward boats to ride in the bow wave, makes an otherworldly association among people and these profoundly wise marine creatures.

The normal dolphin species found in New Zealand's waters likewise incorporate the bottlenose dolphin, known for its unmistakable dorsal balance and perky jokes. The Marlborough Sounds, an organization of indented stream valleys at the northern tip of the South Island, is a locale where bottlenose dolphins successive the protected waters, offering a charming encounter for those investigating the many-sided sounds.

The Hector's dolphin, the littlest and most uncommon dolphin species on the planet, is endemic to New Zealand. Conspicuous by its adjusted dorsal blade and unmistakable high contrast markings, the Hector's dolphin occupies the seaside waters of the South Island. Akaroa Harbor, shaped in the pit of a wiped out fountain of liquid magma, is a famous area for experiencing these minute dolphins right at home.

Marine vertebrate experiences in New Zealand stretch out past whales and dolphins to incorporate seals and ocean lions. The fur seal, a typical sight along the country's rough shorelines, luxuriates in the sun and explores the waves with dexterous effortlessness. Seal settlements, like those on the Otago Landmass, give chances to noticing the communications and ways of behaving of these marine warm blooded animals right at home.

Ocean lions, with their particular stubbles and vigorous bodies, are another species that calls New Zealand home. The subantarctic Auckland Islands, found south of the South Island, have a populace of New Zealand ocean lions. These islands, described by their tough territory and desolate scenes, give a remote and flawless living space for this imperiled ocean lion species.

The marine avian life in New Zealand is similarly different and enrapturing, with seabird provinces spotting the beach front scenes. Gooney birds, with their noteworthy wingspans, are notorious occupants of the country's subantarctic islands. The Imperial Gooney bird, the biggest of the gooney bird species, breeds on Taiaroa Head close to Dunedin, giving an uncommon chance to bird lovers to observe these glorious seabirds in flight.

Penguins, known for their charming waddle and lively ways of behaving, are an esteemed piece of New Zealand's marine life. The yellow-peered toward penguin, otherwise called hoiho in Maori, is a one of a kind and endemic animal varieties that possesses the beach front locales of the South Island and Stewart Island. Perceived by its yellow eye band and unmistakable yellow markings, the yellow-looked at penguin is one of the most uncommon penguin species worldwide.

Oamaru, on the east bank of the South Island, is home to a state of yellow-looked at penguins, giving a safeguarded climate to these imperiled birds. Preservation endeavors, including hunter control and natural surroundings reclamation, expect to protect the rearing locales and scrounging grounds of the yellow-looked at penguin, guaranteeing the endurance of this magnetic species for people in the future.

The little blue penguin, the littlest penguin species, is one more occupant of New Zealand's seaside waters. States of minimal blue penguins are spread around the nation's shores, frequently settling in regular tunnels or man-made structures. The Oamaru Blue Penguin Province, a famous vacation spot, offers a vivid encounter for guests to observe the daily return of these slight penguins to their seaside homes.

The Fiordland Peaked Penguin, known for its unmistakable yellow peak and striking facial markings, breeds in the thick rainforests of the Fiordland locale. Milford Sound, a fjord inside Fiordland Public Park, is a territory for these special penguins, and fortunate guests might get a brief look at them along the fjord's rough shores.

New Zealand's obligation to marine preservation is clear in different drives pointed toward safeguarding the country's novel marine biodiversity. Marine stores, like those in the Hauraki Bay and the Narrows of Islands, add to the safeguarding of basic natural surroundings and the recovery of fish populaces. The Division of Protection (DOC) assumes a focal part in observing and overseeing marine stores, guaranteeing the economical utilization of marine assets.

Protection programs likewise address the dangers presented by presented hunters, like rodents and stoats, to seabird and penguin provinces. Hunter free drives, driven by local area commitment and mechanical development, plan to establish conditions where local species can flourish without the consistent tension of predation.

Environmental change, with its related effects on ocean temperature and sea fermentation, presents difficulties to marine life around the world. New Zealand, as a Pacific island country, is powerless against the impacts of environmental change on its marine biological systems. Observing and research programs, in a joint effort with global accomplices, look to comprehend and moderate the effects of environmental change on the country's marine biodiversity.

3.3 Discuss the importance of sustainable marine practices and conservation efforts.

The significance of manageable marine practices and protection endeavors couldn't possibly be more significant in that frame of mind of the worldwide environmental scene. As humankind wrestles with the mind boggling difficulties presented by environmental change, overfishing, contamination, and natural surroundings debasement, the requirement for proactive measures to shield our seas has become progressively pressing. In the extraordinary sea climate of New Zealand, encompassed by unblemished blue waters and a rich embroidery of marine life, the meaning of manageable marine practices is amplified, mirroring a more extensive worldwide basic to safeguard the well-being and biodiversity of our seas.

Feasible marine practices incorporate a scope of methodologies pointed toward guaranteeing the mindful use and the board of marine assets. At the very front of these practices is supportable fisheries the board, a basic part in keeping up with the fragile equilibrium of marine environments. In New Zealand, where fishing has profound social and financial roots, the execution of supportable fishing rehearses is central to safeguarding both the soundness of the seas and the jobs of beach front networks.

The Share The executives Framework (QMS), laid out in New Zealand in 1986, remains as a spearheading illustration of supportable fisheries the board. Under the QMS, fish stocks are painstakingly observed, and quantities are set to forestall overfishing and consumption of target species.

This approach perceives the interconnectedness of marine species and intends to keep up with the natural respectability of the marine climate. The cooperative endeavors of government organizations, researchers, and the fishing business have added to the outcome of the QMS in advancing supportability and guaranteeing the drawn out suitability of New Zealand's fisheries.

Marine safeguarded regions (MPAs) assume an essential part in moderating biodiversity, safeguarding basic natural surroundings, and encouraging the versatility of marine biological systems. In New Zealand, an organization of marine stores has been laid out to give safe-havens to marine life, permitting species to flourish without the tensions of fishing and other anthropogenic exercises. The foundation of marine stores in the Hauraki Bay, the Cove of Islands, and other key areas adds to the preservation of fish populaces, improves biological system wellbeing, and gives important experiences to logical exploration.

Protection endeavors in New Zealand stretch out past customary ways to deal with incorporate imaginative answers for relieving the effect of presented hunters on local marine species. The destruction of intrusive species, like rodents and stoats, from hunter free islands intends to establish conditions where seabirds and penguins can raise and prosper without the danger of predation. These preservation drives embody the obligation to reestablishing the normal equilibrium and safeguarding the novel biodiversity that characterizes New Zealand's marine biological systems.

The meaning of feasible marine practices in New Zealand is profoundly entwined with Maori social qualities and the idea of kaitiakitanga, or guardianship. For Maori people group, the sea isn't simply an asset yet a living element to be regarded and safeguarded. The obligation to really focus on the land and ocean, gave over through ages, lines up with the standards of economical asset the board and highlights the all encompassing association among individuals and the climate.

Conventional Maori fishing rehearses, established in reasonable standards, underscore the significance of taking just the thing is required and rewarding the climate. The utilization of customary information, went down through oral practices, adds profundity to present day preservation endeavors and gives an extension between native insight and contemporary science. The mix of Maori viewpoints in marine protection drives mirrors an acknowledgment of the social meaning of the seas and the requirement for cooperative methodologies that regard both environmental and social qualities.

New Zealand's obligation to reasonable marine practices is additionally exemplified by its authority in worldwide drives pointed toward tending to more extensive ecological difficulties.

The nation effectively partakes in peaceful accords and shows, like the Unified Countries Practical Advancement Objective 14 (Life Beneath Water), which highlights the worldwide obligation to moderate and economically utilize the seas. Through discretionary channels and cooperative organizations, New Zealand adds to the turn of events and execution of strategies that advance reasonable marine practices on a worldwide scale.

The effect of environmental change on marine biological systems presents an extra layer of intricacy to the difficulties looked by New Zealand and the worldwide local area. Climbing ocean temperatures, sea fermentation, and changes in weather conditions have significant ramifications for marine life and the sensitive equilibrium of biological systems. Accordingly, New Zealand has embraced versatile methodologies that perceive the interconnected idea of environmental change and marine preservation.

The Blue Belt Program, a New Zealand-drove drive, looks to upgrade marine insurance inside the country's elite financial zone (EEZ). This drive lines up with the more extensive objective of making marine safeguarded regions that go about as safe-havens for biodiversity, support zones against environmental change effects, and center points for logical exploration. By consolidating protection endeavors with environment versatility procedures, New Zealand shows a ground breaking way to deal with marine administration that recognizes the diverse difficulties presented by natural change.

Plastic contamination, an unavoidable issue influencing seas universally, is a point of convergence of marine preservation endeavors in New Zealand. The nation has executed measures to lessen single-use plastics, further develop squander the board frameworks, and raise public mindfulness about the effect of plastic on marine conditions. Local area drove ocean side clean-ups and instructive projects add to a culture of natural stewardship, underlining the aggregate liability to address the underlying drivers of plastic contamination.

The Hauraki Bay, an oceanic entryway to Auckland and a locale of environmental and social importance, epitomizes the crossing point of economical marine practices and protection endeavors. The Bay, home to a different scope of marine species and territories, faces difficulties like territory corruption, overfishing, and the effect of urbanization. Drives like the Ocean Change - Tai Timu Tai Pari marine spatial arrangement intend to address these difficulties through cooperative direction, supportable administration rehearses, and the joining of social qualities into marine administration.

The outcome of maintainable marine practices and protection endeavors relies on viable coordinated effort between government offices, logical foundations, non-legislative associations, nearby networks, and native people groups. The participatory idea of marine protection drives, exemplified by co-the board game plans and local area based projects, cultivates a feeling of shared liability and responsibility for assets.

Schooling and public mindfulness assume a significant part in advancing feasible marine practices. Outreach programs, school drives, and mindfulness crusades plan to advise the general population about the significance regarding marine protection, the effect of human exercises on seas, and the job people can play in encouraging positive change. By developing a feeling of ecological obligation and enabling networks to participate in preservation endeavors, these instructive drives add to a culture of manageability that rises above ages.

CHAPTER 4

"Maori Myths and Legends"

Maori fantasies and legends, well established in the social texture of the native Maori individuals of New Zealand, weave an embroidery of rich stories that enlighten the starting points of the land, the universe, and the multifaceted associations between the regular and powerful domains. These accounts, went down through ages by means of oral practices, act as enthralling stories as well as typify significant illustrations, social qualities, and an otherworldly comprehension of the world.

At the core of Maori cosmology is the creation fantasy, which relates the beginning of the universe and the introduction of the land known as Aotearoa, the Maori name for New Zealand. The story starts with the basic guardians, Ranginui, the sky father, and Papatuanuku, the earth mother, who lay secured in a warm hug, their association encompassing the world in obscurity. Their various posterity, the divine beings and goddesses, stayed in the confined space between their folks.

The god Tane Mahuta, loaded up with a longing to carry light and space to the world, coordinated an arrangement to isolate his folks.

With enormous strength and assurance, Tane pushed against his dad, Ranginui, and his mom, Papatuanuku, making space and permitting light to enter. The division of the sky and earth achieved the introduction of the world as far as we might be concerned, with Tane Mahuta expecting the job of the lord of woodlands and birds, representing the nurturing power of nature.

Tane's formation of humankind is one more focal topic in Maori folklore. The goddess Hineahuone, shaped by Tane from the dirt of Papatuanuku, turned into the main lady. Tane reinvigorated her, and from their association, humankind was conceived. This fantasy highlights the close association among people and the land, accentuating the equal connection among individuals and the normal world.

The Polynesian guide and pioneer Kupe assume a huge part in Maori folklore, credited with the revelation of Aotearoa. As indicated by legend, Kupe left on a thinking for even a second to journey across the Pacific Sea, pursuing an enormous octopus named Te Wheke-a-Muturangi. The pursuit took him to the far off shores of New Zealand, where he named different milestones and laid out a way for later relocations. Kupe's journeys and navigational ability are praised in Maori culture, featuring the nautical practices that formed the character of the Maori public.

The notable waka (kayak) includes conspicuously in Maori folklore, representing both viable and otherworldly parts of the way of life. The extraordinary relocation waka, like the Aotea, Mataatua, and Tainui, conveyed the precursors of the Maori to Aotearoa, and their accounts are woven into the texture of the land. The waka likewise fills in as a figurative vessel for life's excursion, addressing the interconnectedness of the past, present, and future.

Quite possibly of the most loved figure in Maori folklore is Maui, a comedian legend whose exploits are both engaging and significant. Maui, conceived rashly and cast into the sea by his mom, was embraced and raised by the divine beings. His trying deeds incorporate fishing up the North Island, easing back the sun to protract the days, and endeavoring to accomplish everlasting status by overcoming Hine-nui-te-po, the goddess of death.

In the narrative of Maui's fishing trip, he and his siblings leave on an excursion to catch the extraordinary fish, Tinirau. Maui projects his enchanted snare, which he molds from the jawbone of his grandma, Murirangawhenua. At the point when the fish is gotten, it turns into the North Island of New Zealand. This fantasy gives a history to the actual land, building up the Maori perspective that interfaces the regular habitat to the deeds of their incredible precursors.

Maui's endeavor to vanquish demise by entering the goddess Hine-nui-te-po's belly is a story of exorbitant pride and outcome. Maui, looking to change passing into a simple condition of obviousness, is eventually impeded when a little bird, the tomtit, illuminates Hine-nui-te-po of his arrangement. As Maui endeavors to go through the goddess, he is squashed, denoting the certainty and perpetual quality of death. This legend mirrors the Maori affirmation of the regular patterns of life and the sacredness of the equilibrium inside the universe.

The practices of the haka, a strong and emblematic dance, are established in Maori folklore and act as a unique articulation of social personality. The haka includes different structures, from war moves to stately exhibitions, and is portrayed by cadenced reciting, stepping, and forceful stances. These moves frequently portray hereditary stories, conjuring the spirits of the land and predecessors to loan strength and solidarity to the entertainers.

The Maori respect their parentage with incredible worship, and the whakapapa (genealogical graphs) follow the lineage of people back to the unbelievable ancestors of the Maori public. Whakapapa isn't only a rundown of names yet a dynamic and living association that ties people to their predecessors, the land, and the otherworldly domain. Every family or iwi (clan) has its interesting whakapapa, and the recitation of these genealogical lines fills in as a formal confirmation of personality and having a place.

The idea of tapu and noa, fundamental to Maori conviction frameworks, shapes the comprehension of holiness and the collaborations between the otherworldly and actual domains. Tapu means the sacrosanct and the confined, incorporating items, spots, and people instilled with profound importance. Noticing tapu includes regarding these holy components and sticking to customs to keep up with equilibrium and congruity.

On the other hand, noa addresses the customary or the regular. To change from tapu to noa, customs, for example, karakia (spells) are performed to lift the holiness. Understanding and exploring the limits among tapu and noa is fundamental in Maori culture, as it administers rehearses connected with birth, demise, and ordinary cooperations.

The figure of the tohunga, or master professional, holds a urgent job in Maori society, filling in as a store of information, profound direction, and useful abilities. Tohunga had particular information in different areas, including cutting, route, mending, and the understanding of heavenly signs. Their aptitude was gone down through ages, guaranteeing the congruity of customary thinking and practices.

The Whare Wananga, or place of learning, was an establishment where tohunga granted information to starts, encouraging a profound comprehension of cosmology, folklore, and the complexities of day to day existence. The advancing inside the Whare Wananga was frequently elusive, open just to those considered commendable and focused on maintaining the consecrated information.

Tangihanga, the Maori burial service ritual, is a serious and elaborate function that respects the departed and gives a structure to lamenting. The custom includes the social event of the local area, the reciting of karakia, and the sharing of anecdotes about the left. The departed is customarily let go in a cut wooden coffin, and the ceremonies related with death and entombment are directed by standards of tapu and noa.

The profound component of Maori fantasies and legends is interlaced with the regular world, as hereditary creatures are frequently connected with normal components, scenes, and heavenly bodies. Te Ika-a-Maui, the North Island, is exemplified as the incredible fish got by Maui, while Te Waka-a-Maui, the South Island, addresses Maui's kayak. The heavenly bodies, like Rona the Moon, are enlivened with human characteristics and take part in the grandiose dance of Maori folklore.

The hallowed Mount Taranaki, a stratovolcano on the North Island, includes unmistakably in Maori folklore as the froze collection of Taranaki, one of the mountains related with the basic guardians Ranginui and Papatuanuku. The encompassing scene, waterways, and geographical highlights are frequently connected to the endeavors and excursions of legendary creatures, making a profoundly interconnected story that attaches the land to its otherworldly legacy.

In the perplexing and layered stories of Maori folklore, the idea of atua envelops a pantheon of divine beings and goddesses, each epitomizing explicit characteristics and jobs. Tangaroa, the divine force of the ocean, is worshipped as a watchman of marine life, while Tawhirimatea, the lord of wind and tempests, states his strength in the domain of climate. These atua address powers of nature and parts of the universe, mirroring the Maori comprehension of the reliance between the human, normal, and otherworldly domains.

The Maori social renaissance, which picked up speed in the last 50% of the twentieth hundred years, assumed a critical part in reviving conventional expressions, language, and narrating. The fuse of Maori fantasies and legends into contemporary imaginative articulations, including cutting, winding around, and visual expressions, highlights the continuous importance of these stories in molding social personality and cultivating a feeling of coherence with the past.

The idea of mana, a profound power or power, penetrates Maori folklore and mixes the regular world with sacrosanct importance. The connection among people and their current circumstance is portrayed by corresponding trades of mana, where the land gives solidarity to individuals, and consequently, individuals maintain the otherworldly equilibrium through customs and dependable stewardship.

The Whare Nui, or meeting house, is a focal component in Maori people group, filling in as a space for get-togethers, functions, and the transmission of social information. The unpredictably cut façade of the Whare Nui frequently portrays tribal figures and legendary scenes, outwardly portraying the tales that interface the local area to its underlying foundations. The gathering house remains as a demonstration of the persevering through presence of Maori legends in daily existence.

The custom of narrating, typified in the specialty of whaikorero (speech), guarantees the oral transmission of Maori fantasies and legends across ages. Whaikorero is a stately type of discourse that consolidates language, motion, and sound to convey familial stories, express regard, and certify social qualities. The specialty of whaikorero embodies the dynamic and living nature of Maori folklore inside the contemporary setting.

Maori fantasies and legends comprise an energetic and essential part of New Zealand's social legacy, giving a significant comprehension of the land's starting points, the connections among people and the climate, and the otherworldly aspects that shape Maori personality. These stories are not static relics of the past but rather living articulations that keep on advancing, adjust, and reverberate in the hearts and brains of the Maori public. The tales of creation, divine beings, legends, and predecessors act as a social compass, directing the Maori people group in exploring the intricacies of the cutting edge world while keeping a profound association with the immortal insight implanted in their mythic practices.

4.1 Delve into the rich cultural heritage of the Maori people.

The rich social legacy of the Maori public, the native Polynesian occupants of New Zealand, envelops an embroidery of customs, customs, works of art, and otherworldly convictions that have developed over hundreds of years. From their appearance in Aotearoa (New Zealand) a while back to the current day, the Maori have kept a profound association with their genealogical roots, making an energetic social scene that reflects flexibility, imagination, and a significant comprehension of their current circumstance.

At the center of Maori culture is the idea of whakapapa, a genealogical structure that follows people's family line back to the legendary beginnings of the Maori public. Whakapapa isn't just a rundown of names however a dynamic and living association that ties people to their progenitors, the land, and the profound domain. Every family or iwi (clan) has its novel whakapapa, and the recitation of these tribal lines fills in as a ceremonial confirmation of personality and having a place.

The Marae, a focal social occasion place for Maori people group, is an actual indication of whakapapa and social character. Comprising of a collective region, a wharenui (meeting house), and a wharekai (feasting corridor), the Marae fills in as a space for services, gatherings, and far-reaching developments. The complicatedly cut wharenui frequently portrays genealogical figures and legendary scenes, outwardly portraying the accounts that associate the local area to its foundations.

The customary Maori welcoming, the hongi, represents the trading of breath and the blending of spirits, building up the interconnectedness of people inside the whakapapa system. This standard demonstration of squeezing noses and temples together typifies the substance of Maori accommodation and recognizes the common family that joins individuals.

The Whaikorero, or rhetoric, is an exceptionally esteemed and stylized type of discourse inside Maori culture. This specialty of public communicating in includes language, motion, and sound to convey familial accounts, express regard, and avow social qualities. Whaikorero is acted in different settings, from formal services on the Marae to local meetings, and is a crucial method for safeguarding and sending social information across ages.

Tikanga Maori, the standard practices and conventions that guide conduct, are profoundly implanted in Maori culture. These conventions administer connections inside the local area, customs, and associations with the climate. Noticing Tikanga Maori is fundamental for keeping up with equilibrium and concordance, recognizing tapu (holiness) and noa (normal), and maintaining the standards of correspondence and regard.

The idea of mana, a profound power or power, pervades Maori culture and implants the regular world with sacrosanct importance. People, places, and items can have mana, and the connection between them includes proportional trades of this otherworldly power. The whare tapere, conventional places of diversion, were spaces where exhibitions, narrating, and imaginative articulations were instilled with mana, commending the inventiveness and social personality of the local area.

Maori creative articulations, including cutting, winding around, and inking, are unmistakable structures that typify social stories and imagery. The craft of whakairo (cutting) is portrayed by mind boggling designs, adapted figures, and themes that convey accounts of lineage, folklore, and the normal world. Whakairo decorates meeting houses, kayaks, and regular items, filling in as a visual language that associates the material and otherworldly domains.

The Ta Moko, or customary Maori tattoo, holds significant social importance as a noticeable articulation of personality, status, and whakapapa. Each moko is remarkable, mirroring the singular's family history, accomplishments, and valuable encounters. The method involved with getting a moko is a hallowed and stately demonstration, frequently joined by ceremonies and whakapapa recitations. The multifaceted examples and plans of the moko recount to a visual story that turns into a living demonstration of the individual's association with their social legacy.

Kapa Haka, the customary performing specialties of the Maori, envelops a scope of expressive structures, including melody, dance, and reciting. Kapa Haka is a strong method for narrating, conveying stories of the land, progenitors, and verifiable occasions. Exhibitions frequently highlight the haka, a dynamic and cadenced dance joined by vocal articulations and motions. The haka, with its different structures, fills in as a social seal that reverberates universally, addressing the strength, pride, and solidarity of the Maori public.

Waiata, or tunes, are essential to Maori social articulations, filling in as a vehicle for narrating, mourn, festivity, and articulation of feelings. Each waiata conveys its novel tune and verses, mirroring the different parts of Maori life and social encounters.

Waiata can be performed independently or on the whole, and the cadenced hints of customary instruments, like the poi (a ball on a string), add profundity and reverberation to the melodic articulations.

The Haka, maybe the most globally perceived part of Maori culture, has risen above its conventional setting to turn into an image of New Zealand character. Whether performed before a rugby match, at a comprehensive development, or on the worldwide stage, the haka reverberates as a strong articulation of Maori pride, strength, and versatility. The All Blacks, New Zealand's public rugby crew, play had a critical impact in promoting the haka on the world stage, displaying the social wealth of the Maori legacy.

The protection and rejuvenation of the Maori language, Te Reo Maori, are fundamental to endeavors in defending social personality. Te Reo Maori, an Eastern Polynesian language, fills in as a vault of social information, oral practices, and profound ideas. Language rejuvenation drives mean to guarantee the intergenerational transmission of Te Reo Maori, perceiving its fundamental job in keeping areas of strength for a unique Maori social character.

The Toi Maori development, a drive advancing Maori expressions and culture, plays had a vital impact in encouraging the renewal and contemporary articulation of conventional imaginative structures. Toi Maori envelops visual expressions, performing expressions, scholarly expressions, and conventional information, giving a stage to craftsmen to interface with their social legacy and offer their manifestations with a more extensive crowd. Through shows, celebrations, and cooperative tasks, Toi Maori adds to the continuous advancement of Maori imaginative articulations.

The connection between the Maori public and the regular habitat is profoundly otherworldly and structures a vital piece of their social personality. The idea of kaitiakitanga, or guardianship, stresses the obligation of people and networks to really focus on the land, waters, and assets. The customary acts of supportable asset the executives, for example, the occasional gathering of kai (food) and the utilization of conventional information in protection endeavors, mirror the Maori obligation to natural stewardship.

The Whanganui Stream, the third-longest waterway in New Zealand, holds unique importance in Maori culture, as it is viewed as a precursor with its own lawful personality. In 2017, the Whanganui Stream acquired lawful personhood, a notable acknowledgment that lines up with Maori cosmology, where normal elements are viewed as interconnected with human prosperity. This lawful acknowledgment embodies the combination of customary Maori points of view with contemporary legitimate structures.

The idea of Turangawaewae, a spot to stand, epitomizes the possibility of a hallowed and familial association with a particular land or spot. Turangawaewae fills in as a profound anchor, addressing a feeling of having a place, character, and coherence with the past.

Maori people group frequently express their association with Turangawaewae through the foundation of Papakainga, public living regions that cultivate a feeling of local area, connection, and social congruity.

The Arrangement of Waitangi, endorsed in 1840 between the English Crown and Maori bosses, holds tremendous verifiable and contemporary importance in molding the connection between the Maori public and the New Zealand government. The Settlement was expected to lay out an organization, safeguard Maori freedoms, and empower serene concurrence. In any case, varying translations and breaks of the Settlement over the long run have prompted continuous conversations and discussions for equity, acknowledgment, and the assurance of Maori privileges.

Contemporary Maori activism and backing endeavors address social, financial, and natural issues confronting the local area. The resurgence of social pride, combined with a promise to civil rights, has prompted drives that look to address variations in wellbeing, schooling, and portrayal. Maori voices pushing for acknowledgment, compromise, and the reclamation of social privileges add to the continuous discourse about the spot of the Maori nation inside the more extensive New Zealand society.

The getting through tradition of the Maori Legion, the 28th Maori Contingent, in The Second Great War is a demonstration of the fearlessness, penance, and responsibility of Maori troopers who served their country. The legion, contained fundamentally of Maori volunteers, assumed an essential part in different venues of the conflict. Their commitments are honored through commemorations, haka exhibitions, and a profound feeling of public pride.

The rich social legacy of the Maori public is a living and dynamic power that keeps on forming the personality of New Zealand. From the old practices of whakapapa and Tikanga Maori to the contemporary articulations of Kapa Haka and Toi Maori, Maori culture represents versatility, variation, and a significant association with the regular and profound domains. The continuous endeavors to revive Te Reo Maori, declare social freedoms, and address verifiable treacheries highlight the versatility of the Maori public in exploring the intricacies of the cutting edge world while keeping a profound and persevering through association with their tribal legacy. As watchmen of their territory and culture, the Maori public epitomize a one of a kind and lively social inheritance that enhances New Zealand as well as the worldwide embroidery of human variety and legacy.

4.2 Explore traditional myths and legends that are woven into the landscape and landmarks.

The customary fantasies and legends of New Zealand, profoundly interweaved with the nation's scene and milestones, weave a story embroidery that mirrors the rich social legacy of the Maori public.

These accounts, went down through ages by means of oral customs, not just give an interesting look into the beginnings of the land yet in addition pervade regular highlights with profound importance and social personality.

One of the primary legends in Maori cosmology is the narrative of creation, which starts with the base guardians Ranginui (the sky father) and Papatuanuku (the earth mother) secured in a warm hug. Their youngsters, the divine beings and goddesses, stayed in the confined space among them, and the world was dove into murkiness. Tane Mahuta, the divine force of timberlands and birds, imagined an arrangement to isolate his folks and carry light and space to the world.

With gigantic strength and assurance, Tane pushed against Ranginui and Papatuanuku, making space and permitting light to enter. This detachment denoted the introduction of the world and laid out the underpinnings of Aotearoa, the place that is known for the long white cloud, presently known as New Zealand. Tane Mahuta, playing accepted his part as the divine force of backwoods, reinvigorated the main lady, Hineahuone, framed from the dirt of Papatuanuku. From their association, humankind was conceived, stressing the interconnectedness of people and the normal world.

The legend of Maui, a respected and wicked figure in Maori folklore, is unpredictably connected to the scene and milestones of New Zealand. Maui, conceived rashly and cast into the sea by his mom, was taken on and raised by the divine beings. His trying adventures incorporate fishing up the North Island, easing back the sun to extend the days, and endeavoring to accomplish everlasting status by entering the goddess Hine-nui-te-po's belly.

In the tale of Maui's fishing trip, he and his siblings set out on an excursion to catch the extraordinary fish, Tinirau. Maui projects his otherworldly snare, designed from the jawbone of his grandma Murirangawhenua, and the fish turns into the North Island of New Zealand. This fantasy not just gives a history to the land yet in addition mirrors the Maori perspective that associates the common habitat to the deeds of their unbelievable predecessors.

Maui's endeavor to vanquish demise is one more fantasy profoundly imbued in the scene. Looking to change demise into a condition of obviousness, Maui tries to go through the goddess Hine-nui-te-po. In any case, his arrangement is impeded when a little bird, the tomtit, illuminates the goddess, prompting Maui's end. This fantasy fills in as a powerful sign of the certainty and lastingness of death, underlining the cyclic idea of life inside Maori cosmology.

The notorious waka, or kayak, includes conspicuously in Maori folklore and assumes an emblematic part in the social scene. The incredible relocation waka, like the Aotea, Mataatua, and Tainui, conveyed the progenitors of the Maori to Aotearoa. The names of these waka are scratched into the aggregate memory of the Maori public, turning out to be important for the social texture that associates them to their genealogical roots.

The Whanganui Stream, the third-longest waterway in New Zealand, is exemplified in Maori folklore as a precursor with its own lawful character. The stream holds extraordinary importance as a living substance, mirroring the interconnectedness of the regular and profound domains. In 2017, the Whanganui Stream acquired lawful personhood, denoting a momentous acknowledgment lined up with Maori cosmology, where normal substances are viewed as interconnected with human prosperity.

Mount Taranaki, a stratovolcano on the North Island, includes unmistakably in Maori folklore as the froze collection of Taranaki, one of the mountains related with the base guardians Ranginui and Papatuanuku. The encompassing scene, streams, and geographical highlights are frequently connected to the endeavors and excursions of legendary creatures, making a profoundly inter-connected story that attaches the land to its otherworldly legacy.

The holiness of Mount Taranaki is additionally accentuated by its relation-ship with the celebrated bird-man Tawhiri, the lord of wind and tempests. As indicated by legend, Tawhiri, maddened by the detachment of his folks Rang-inui and Papatuanuku, released his rage on his kin. Escaping from the vicious-ness, Taranaki looked for shelter in the focal North Island, making the scene as he moved. The particular state of Mount Taranaki, with its even cone, is viewed as a demonstration of the profound meaning of the mountain.

Lake Taupo, the biggest lake in New Zealand, is attached to the fantasy of Ngatoroirangi, a consecrated minister and pilot. As per legend, Ngatoroirangi and his sisters traveled to Aotearoa from Hawaiki in the genealogical waka Arawa. While investigating the focal North Island, Ngatoroirangi climbed Mount Tongariro and became abandoned by a blizzard. In a frantic supplication for help, he presented strong chants, calling fire from the hidden world. This act saved Ngatoroirangi as well as shaped the geothermal action in the district, including the fountains and underground aquifers around Lake Taupo.

The geothermal miracles of Rotorua, a district on the North Island, are saturated with Maori folklore and are related with the genealogical figures Whakaue and Te Pupu. The emission of the Te Pupu Spring is said to have been brought about by the sorrow of Whakaue, who lost her better half in fight. The warm action in Rotorua is viewed as a declaration of the feelings and powers underneath the World's surface, mirroring the interconnectedness of the normal and otherworldly domains.

The legends encompassing the Southern Alps, a glorious mountain range that navigates the South Island, are established in the legendary story of Aoraki and his siblings. As per the fantasy, Aoraki and his siblings were changed into the Southern Alps after their waka, Te Waka o Aoraki, became abandoned and frozen in the sea. The pinnacles of the Southern Alps, including Aoraki/Mount Cook, are viewed as the actual exemplification of the genealogical creatures, interfacing the land to the divine domain.

The seaside bluffs of Cape Reinga, situated at the northern tip of the North Island, hold profound otherworldly importance in Maori folklore. It is accepted that the spirits of the departed Maori travel to Cape Reinga to withdraw from the human world and start their excursion to the genealogical country of Hawaiki. The desolate scene and the gathering of the Tasman Ocean and Pacific Sea mark the sacrosanct takeoff point, representing the change from life to the hereafter.

The Waipoua Woodland, home to old kauri trees, is saturated with Maori folklore and fills in as a safe-haven for the spirits of the progenitors. Tane Mahuta, the lord of timberlands, is related with the powerful kauri tree of a similar name. The transcending presence of Tane Mahuta in the backwoods mirrors the veneration for the normal world and its association with the heavenly inside Maori cosmology.

The Pouakai Reach, arranged in the Egmont Public Park on the North Island, is connected to the amazing bird-man Pouakai. As per Maori folklore, the Pouakai is a monster bird that threatened the district, going after people. The bumpy territory of the Pouakai Reach is viewed as the resting spot of this legendary bird, adding to the scene's social importance.

Lake Rotomahana, known for its underground aquifers and geothermal highlights, is related with the Pink and White Porches, normal arrangements that were once viewed as the eighth miracle of the world. The Patios were accepted to be the flight of stairs to the sky, made by the goddesses Papatuanuku and Wairaka. Tragically, the emission of Mount Tarawera in 1886 covered the Patios, modifying the scene and abandoning a lowered social fortune.

The legends of Hawaiki, the familial country from which the Maori are accepted to have relocated to Aotearoa, are implanted in the social awareness. While Hawaiki stays a legendary spot, its importance lies in the hereditary associations and the excursion of the waka across the tremendous Pacific Sea to the shores of New Zealand. The oral customs and navigational ability of the Polynesian predecessors highlight the getting through tradition of Hawaiki as an image of social beginning.

The Maori idea of tapu and noa, integral to their conviction framework, further saturates the scene and milestones with otherworldly importance. Tapu means the consecrated and the limited, incorporating articles, spots, and people instilled with otherworldly importance. Noticing tapu includes regarding these sacrosanct components and sticking to customs to keep up with equilibrium and amicability. On the other hand, noa addresses the standard or the regular, and customs are performed to lift the tapu and progress to a condition of noa.

The conservation of tapu is obvious in the Maori practice of rahui, a transitory denial or limitation put on an area to permit assets to recover.

This standard way to deal with asset the executives mirrors the profound association between social convictions and ecological stewardship. The tapu related with specific tourist spots fills in as a sign of the corresponding connection between the Maori public and their regular environmental factors.

The customary fantasies and legends woven into the scene and milestones of New Zealand are vital to the social personality of the Maori public. These stories, established in cosmology, creation, and hereditary excursions, give a significant comprehension of the interconnectedness between the regular and otherworldly domains. The actual scenes become archives of social memory, welcoming investigation and translation that goes past the actual elements to uncover the layers of significance implanted in the social legacy of Aotearoa. The persevering through presence of these fantasies in the contemporary cognizance of the Maori public highlights the strength and progression of a social heritage profoundly entwined with the land they call home.

4.3 Discuss the importance of the Maori language (Te Reo) and the preservation of cultural traditions.

The Maori language, Te Reo, remains as a social fortune and a basic part of the character and legacy of the Maori nation in New Zealand. The conservation and renewal of Te Reo Maori are fundamental to endeavors pointed toward supporting social practices, cultivating intergenerational associations, and keeping an unmistakable Maori voice in the cutting edge world.

Te Reo Maori fills in as something beyond a method for correspondence; it is a vault of social information, oral practices, and otherworldly ideas. The language conveys the narratives of the land, the insight of predecessors, and the perplexing subtleties of Maori cosmology. Through Te Reo, the Maori public express their perspective, convey the wealth of their social legacy, and lucid the associations between the regular and profound domains.

Endeavors to safeguard Te Reo Maori are well established in an acknowledgment of its importance as a living epitome of Maori personality. The language capabilities as a unique power that shapes social communications, social articulations, and the connection among people and their current circumstance. It is a vessel through which the Maori public convey their particular perspective, values, and viewpoints on the world.

The authentic direction of Te Reo Maori mirrors the effect of colonization and the difficulties looked by native dialects around the world. With the appearance of European pioneers in the mid nineteenth 100 years, the burden of English as the prevailing language, combined with strategies putting the utilization of Te Reo, prompted a decrease in its use down. The outcomes of these strategies, alongside cultural movements, brought about a slow disintegration of the language, jeopardizing its endurance.

In light of these difficulties, the Maori people group left on an excursion of renewal, perceiving that the conservation of Te Reo is essential to protecting social practices. The foundation of Kohanga Reo, or language homes, during the 1980s denoted a critical achievement in this rejuvenation exertion. Kohanga Reo are youth submersion focuses where kids are presented to Te Reo and Maori social practices since the beginning, cultivating a characteristic and bona fide language procurement process.

The obligation to reviving Te Reo Maori picked up additional speed with the foundation of Kura Kaupapa Maori, Maori language inundation schools, giving instruction thanks to Te Reo. These schools offer an all encompassing way to deal with picking up, coordinating language, culture, and scholarly subjects inside a Maori social structure. Kura Kaupapa Maori add to language protection as well as act as spaces where social customs are implanted in regular training.

Te Reo Maori's status as an authority language of New Zealand, close by English and New Zealand Communication via gestures, highlights its importance in the public setting. Acknowledgment at the regulative level mirrors a promise to the rejuvenation and standardization of Te Reo inside more extensive society. Different drives, including language rejuvenation projects, assets, and media, add to expanding the perceivability and use of Te Reo in assorted areas.

The festival of Te Wiki o Te Reo Maori (Maori Language Week) every year in New Zealand fills in as a devoted chance to advance and praise the language. During this week, networks take part in a scope of exercises, occasions, and drives that support language use, mindfulness, and learning. Te Wiki o Te Reo Maori fills in as a point of convergence for supporting the significance of Te Reo inside the more extensive public character.

The advanced age has given new roads to language safeguarding and learning. Online stages, language applications, and advanced assets offer open apparatuses for people to draw in with Te Reo Maori. These innovative drives add to separating obstructions to getting the hang of, contacting a more extensive crowd, and cultivating a feeling of network inside the Maori diaspora and then some.

The significance of Te Reo Maori reaches out past semantic contemplations; it is profoundly entwined with the safeguarding of social customs. The language fills in as a key medium through which social information, values, and practices are communicated starting with one age then onto the next. The lavishness of Maori folklore, whakapapa (lineage), and tikanga (customs) is complicatedly woven into the texture of Te Reo, making a phonetic embroidery that mirrors the profundity of Maori social legacy.

Whakapapa, specifically, assumes a pivotal part in the Maori comprehension of character and association with the land.

Te Reo Maori fills in as the vehicle through which genealogical lines are recounted and shared, connecting people to their underlying foundations and attesting their place inside the more extensive whanau (family) and hapu (subclan). The recitation of whakapapa is certainly not a simple identification of names however a living articulation that secures people in the stories of their predecessors and the land.

Tikanga Maori, the standard practices and conventions that administer conduct and cooperations inside the local area, track down their appearance in Te Reo Maori. The language is natural for the presentation of customs, functions, and everyday exercises directed by tikanga. The right utilization of Te Reo guarantees that these social practices are done with accuracy, regard, and adherence to the conventions laid out by the precursors.

The haka, a strong and dynamic type of social articulation, embodies the combination of Te Reo Maori with customary practices. The haka includes different structures, from war moves to stately exhibitions, and is described by musical reciting, stepping, and forceful stances. Te Reo is the vehicle through which the verses and spells of the haka are conveyed, imbuing the presentation with phonetic and social importance.

Te Reo Maori is additionally implanted in the visual expressions, especially whakairo (cutting) and raranga (winding around). The many-sided examples and themes in carvings and weavings frequently convey explicit implications, stories, and familial associations, all expressed through Te Reo. These creative structures act as unmistakable articulations of social personality and add to the dynamic visual language that describes Maori imaginative practices.

The job of Te Reo Maori in cultivating a feeling of having a place and personality is obvious in the idea of Turangawaewae, a spot to stand. The language furnishes people with a semantic anchor to their genealogical terrains and social roots, building up a feeling of coherence and association across ages. Turangawaewae isn't only an actual area yet a profound and etymological space where people track down establishing in their social personality.

The association between Te Reo Maori and the indigenous habitat is significant. The language exemplifies the customary natural information implanted in Maori cosmology, mirroring a cozy comprehension of the land, waters, and heavenly bodies. Te Reo conveys the names, stories, and similitudes that typify the interconnectedness among people and the normal world, adding to the all encompassing perspective of the Maori public.

The transmission of Te Reo Maori inside families, whanau, and networks is an essential part of its conservation. Connections in daily existence, from good tidings to narrating, give potential open doors to language use and learning. The familial climate turns into a supporting space where Te Reo is passed down from older folks to youngsters, encouraging a feeling of coherence and guaranteeing that etymological customs are supported across ages.

The significance of Te Reo Maori isn't restricted to the Maori people group alone; it has more extensive ramifications for the social variety and character of New Zealand all in all. The acknowledgment and regard for Te Reo add to the more extensive objective of making a comprehensive and socially rich society. Embracing semantic variety cultivates a feeling of public pride and recognizes the extraordinary commitments of the Maori nation to the social mosaic of New Zealand.

Challenges in the conservation of Te Reo Maori persevere, and progressing endeavors are expected to address them. These difficulties incorporate the requirement for expanded capability levels, particularly among more youthful ages, and the joining of Te Reo into different circles of public life. Training assumes an essential part in language rejuvenation, and drives to coordinate Te Reo into standard schooling add to its standardization and boundless use.

The significance of Te Reo Maori and the safeguarding of social customs stretch out a long ways past phonetic contemplations. Te Reo is a living demonstration of the social extravagance, versatility, and one of a kind personality of the Maori public. Its protection isn't just about language; about shielding a comprehensive social legacy envelops stories, ceremonies, works of art, and the interconnectedness between individuals, land, and otherworldliness. As Te Reo Maori keeps on tracking down its spot in the computerized age, instructive organizations, and public spaces, it not just enhances the social variety of New Zealand yet in addition remains as a demonstration of the persevering through soul of the Maori public and their obligation to protecting their novel legacy for a long time into the future.

CHAPTER 5

"Adventure Awaits"

"Experience Is standing by"

In the immense and changed scenes of our reality, the expression "Experience Is standing by" resounds as a call to investigate the obscure, embrace difficulties, and find the phenomenal. It catches the pith of the human soul that looks for rush, interest, and the untamed magnificence that lies past the recognizable skyline. Whether scaling transcending tops, navigating thick wildernesses, plunging into the profundities of the sea, or wandering into the core of clamoring urban communities, the commitment of experience calls, welcoming people to leave on an excursion of self-revelation and investigation.

At the core of the explorer's soul is the voracious longing for disclosure, a longing to reveal the mysteries concealed in the furthest reaches of the world. Experience isn't simply an actual pursuit; an outlook embraces the obscure with great enthusiasm, inviting the difficulties and flightiness that accompany wandering into strange domains. It is an affirmation that development, learning, and change frequently happen in the spaces where safe places disappear, supplanted by the elating unexplored world.

Mountain ranges stand as considerable jungle gyms for those looking for the charm of elevation and the magnificence of transcending tops. The Himalayas, delegated by the world's most noteworthy culmination, Mount Everest, embody the soul of experience in the domain of mountaineering. Scaling these levels requests actual ability as well as mental strength, as climbers explore deceptive landscape, face unusual climate, and vanquish their deepest feelings of trepidation. Every climb turns into an individual odyssey, a demonstration of human assurance, and a fellowship with the dazzling force of nature.

Wildernesses, with their lavish coverings and overflowing biodiversity, present a material for an alternate sort of experience — one that unfurls in the midst of the orchestra of untamed life calls and the stir of leaves underneath. The Amazon Rainforest, frequently alluded to as the "Lungs of the Earth," offers a vivid involvement with nature's untamed magnificence. Exploring its winding streams and thick vegetation uncovers a reality where lively parrots take off above, tricky panthers sneak in the shadows, and the sheer variety of life dazzles the faculties. Experience in the wilderness is a hit the dance floor with the musicality of the environment, a sign of the sensitive equilibrium that supports life on our planet.

Underneath the outer layer of the sea lies a domain of secret and miracle, welcoming bold spirits to dive into its profundities. Experience takes on a liquid structure in the submerged scenes of coral reefs, kelp woodlands, and deep fields. Scuba plunging turns into a visa to an existence where bright marine life moves through perfectly clear waters, and lowered caves conceal old mysteries. The Incomparable Obstruction Reef, the world's biggest coral reef framework, is a demonstration of the vivid magnificence of the sea, where experience unfurls in the influence of seagrasses and the delicate influence of anemones.

Urban areas, with their transcending high rises and clamoring roads, offer an alternate sort of experience — an investigation of human creativity, culture, and the dynamic embroidery of metropolitan life. The city turns into a jungle gym for the people who look for the excitement of disclosure in the cadence of day to day existence, the workmanship embellishing back streets, and the kinds of different foods. Tokyo, a city where custom and development combine, epitomizes the metropolitan experience. From the tranquility of old sanctuaries to the neon-lit energy of Akihabara, each corner divulges a feature of a city that throbs with life and entices travelers to plunge into its complexities.

Experience isn't bound to outer scenes alone; it lives inside the domains of the psyche and soul. Abstract excursions through the pages of books, realistic odysseys on the cinema, and the quest for information in scholarly community all epitomize the soul of experience. The composed word turns into a vessel that transports perusers to fantastical domains, verifiable ages, and equal universes. Experience, in this sense, turns into a mission for edification, sympathy, and understanding, as people navigate the scenes of creative mind and keenness.

The charm of experience stretches out past the physical and scholarly domains; it is profoundly interwoven with the close to home scene of the human experience. Love, with its flighty exciting bends in the road, turns into an experience of the heart. Connections, companionships, and associations with others convey the potential for euphoria, disclosure, and shared encounters that characterize the human excursion. Experience, in the domain of feelings, is a festival of weakness, association, and the unfathomable limit of the human heart to investigate the profundities of love and fellowship.

Experience isn't without its difficulties and dangers. It expects mental fortitude to confront the obscure, strength to beat obstructions, and a readiness to embrace inconvenience. It is in the cauldron of affliction that the genuine soul of experience sparkles most splendid. The mountain dweller fighting cruel atmospheric conditions, the pilgrim exploring unfamiliar waters, and the individual venturing into the obscure territory of self-improvement — all represent the victory of the human soul notwithstanding challenges.

In the time of innovation and globalization, the idea of experience has advanced. Virtual scenes, increased reality, and advanced narrating offer new outskirts for investigation. Computer games, with their vivid stories and extensive virtual universes, give a stage to explorers to leave on legendary journeys, tackle perplexes, and communicate with complex characters. The computerized domain turns into a material where the limits among the real world and dream obscure, opening roads for experience in uncommon ways.

The ethos of experience is profoundly implanted chasing after self-improvement and self-disclosure. Each excursion, whether physical or figurative, turns into a mirror mirroring the qualities, shortcomings, and undiscovered possibilities inside. The traveler, in exploring the outside and inner scenes, graphs a course towards a more significant comprehension of themselves and their general surroundings. It is in the pot of investigation that people find aspects of their personality, flexibility, and limit with regards to variation.

The idea of experience stretches out its arms to the enterprising soul — the trailblazers who hope against hope, develop, and diagram new regions in the business scene. Business turns into an excursion laden with vulnerabilities, gambles, and the excitement of making a new thing. The startup organizer exploring unfamiliar market drifts, the visionary testing laid out standards, and the imaginative psyche pushing the limits of advancement — all encapsulate the pioneering experience. It is in the cauldron of business that people make financial worth as well as add to the consistently advancing story of human advancement.

The appeal of experience isn't restricted by age, orientation, or foundation. A widespread call reverberates across ages, societies, and social orders. Youngsters, with their unfathomable interest, typify the most perfect type of the daring soul.

The lawn turns into a wilderness to investigate, a cardboard box changes into a spaceship, and ordinary minutes become legendary experiences in the creative scenes of young life. The soul of experience, when lighted in youth, stays a deep rooted sidekick, developing and adjusting to the changing parts of life.

The idea of experience additionally tracks down reverberation chasing civil rights and activism. Advocates for change explore strange waters, testing laid out standards, and endeavoring to make a world that lines up with standards of value, inclusivity, and equity. The mission for an all the more and humane society turns into an undertaking in itself, set apart by the boldness to defy fundamental issues, the flexibility to endure resistance, and the obligation to molding a superior future for all.

The expression "Experience Is standing by" typifies a well known fact — the natural human craving to investigate, find, and embrace the full range of the human experience. Whether scaling mountains, jumping into the profundities of the sea, exploring clamoring urban communities, or leaving on the experience of self-awareness, the call to investigate the obscure is a demonstration of the persevering through soul of the human excursion. Experience, in the entirety of its structures, turns into a material whereupon people paint the embroidery of their lives — an excursion set apart by interest, boldness, and the resolute conviction that, past each skyline, another experience is standing by.

5.1 Highlight New Zealand's reputation as the adventure capital of the world.

New Zealand, settled in the southwestern Pacific Sea, has procured a merited standing as the experience capital of the world. Its staggering scenes, various environments, and a culture well established in open air pursuits have on the whole changed the country into a jungle gym for adrenaline devotees and nature darlings the same. From the snow-covered pinnacles of the Southern Alps to the immaculate blue waters encompassing its shores, New Zealand's standing as an experience sanctuary is carved into the actual texture of its character.

The Southern Alps, extending across the spine of the South Island, act as the focal point of New Zealand's experience interests. Queenstown, a pleasant retreat town settled on the shores of Lake Wakatipu, has arisen as the undisputed experience capital of the country. Encircled by the superb pinnacles of the Remarkables and the rough scenes of Fiordland, Queenstown is a passage to a variety of heart-beating exercises that have come to characterize the Kiwi soul of experience.

Queenstown's standing as an experience mecca is maybe generally broadly connected with bungee hopping. The Kawarau Scaffold, where the world's most memorable business bungee hop occurred in 1988, still attracts adrenaline junkies anxious to venture out into the turquoise waters of the Kawarau Stream.

The thinking for even a second to can likewise encounter the Nevis Bungy, a stomach-beating 134 meters of drop from a suspended case that hangs high over the Nevis Waterway gorge. These notable leaps exemplify the Kiwi ethos of pushing limits and embracing the invigorating surge of adrenaline.

Past bungee bouncing, Queenstown offers a range of high power exercises. Skydiving permits explorers to jump from airplane and experience the stunning vistas of Lake Wakatipu and the encompassing mountains during a fast drop prior to sending the parachute. The town's sloping landscape gives a characteristic jungle gym to downhill mountain trekking, with trails taking care of riders of all expertise levels. The Queenstown Bicycle Park, settled in the Ben Lomond Save, offers a maze of tracks highlighting bounces, embankments, and specialized plummets, making it a safe house for mountain trekking devotees.

For those attracted to the quietness of the skies, paragliding offers a novel viewpoint of Queenstown's scenes. Drifting easily over the valleys and lakes, paragliders are blessed to receive all encompassing perspectives that progress from elevated glades to dark blue waters, making an encounter that flawlessly mixes thrill with peacefulness. The pair paragliding encounters, directed via prepared pilots, take care of the two fledglings and experienced flyers, guaranteeing that the delight of flight is available to all.

New Zealand's experience notoriety stretches out past Queenstown, arriving at the frosty domains of the Franz Josef and Fox Icy masses on the West Coast. Here, travelers can leave on heli-climbing undertakings, consolidating the adventure of helicopter trips with the striking experience of journeying on antiquated ice sheets. The transcending ice developments, profound precipices, and turquoise meltwater pools make a dreamlike background for investigation, offering an extraordinary mix of high experience and icy disclosure.

The country's North Island, as well, adds to its daring charm. Rotorua, known for its geothermal miracles and Maori culture, is a center for adrenaline-powered exercises. The foaming mud pools and ejecting fountains set up for exceptional encounters, for example, zorbing — a game that includes moving downhill inside a goliath straightforward circle. Zorbing lovers end up turning and tumbling as they explore the undulating scenes, making a chuckling filled experience that opposes gravity.

Rotorua's geothermal action additionally powers the adrenaline surge of wilderness boating on the Kaituna Waterway. The Kaituna flaunts the world's most noteworthy monetarily boated cascade, the Tutea Falls, where adrenaline junkies explore through testing rapids prior to plunging over the 7-meter drop. This mix of geothermal ponders and white-water fervor epitomizes how New Zealand flawlessly incorporates its regular scenes into experience pursuits.

The Tongariro Public Park, an UNESCO World Legacy site on the North Island, offers one more aspect to New Zealand's experience collection. The Tongariro Elevated Crossing, frequently hailed as one of the world's greatest day climbs, navigates a volcanic scene of emotional cavities, emerald lakes, and lunar-like territory. The provoking journey comes full circle with the choice to highest point Mount Ngauruhoe, furnishing all encompassing perspectives that reward explorers with a feeling of achievement and an association with the crude, immaculate excellence of the New Zealand wild.

New Zealand's marine surroundings further add to its standing as an experience objective. The town of Kaikoura, arranged on the northeastern bank of the South Island, is famous for its marine experiences. Here, globe-trotters can leave on whale-watching journeys, where the potential chance to observe the goliath sperm whales breaking the sea's surface is a lowering and sensational experience. The waterfront waters of Kaikoura additionally draw in perky units of gloomy dolphins, offering the opportunity for swimmers to join these astute marine animals right at home.

The Straight of Islands, situated in the northernmost piece of the North Island, gives a picturesque setting to sea experiences. Cruising lovers can explore the straight's perfect waters, investigating detached bays, noteworthy destinations, and the notorious "Opening in the Stone" at Cape Brett. Kayaking journeys offer a more personal association with the marine climate, permitting swashbucklers to paddle through ocean caves, experience marine natural life, and witness the lively shades of the submerged world.

The Waitomo Caverns, with their twisted organizations of underground loads, offer an underground experience enlightened by the delicate gleam of bioluminescent glowworms. Buckling endeavors through the Waitomo Glowworm Caverns divulge a mystical reality where tapered rocks and stalagmites make extraordinary developments, and the brilliance of glowworms changes the caves into a divine scene. Abseiling and dark water boating encounters add a component of fervor to this underground excursion.

Queenstown, Rotorua, Tongariro, Kaikoura, and Waitomo are only a couple of the key objections that add to New Zealand's moniker as the experience capital of the world. The country's different scenes, going from high tops to beach front waters, give a characteristic material to a bunch of experience pursuits. Besides, New Zealand's obligation to maintainable the travel industry guarantees that these experiences are exciting as well as eco-cognizant, protecting the flawless conditions for people in the future of globe-trotters.

The Kiwi culture itself assumes an essential part in forming New Zealand's standing as an experience safe house. The soul of "kiwi inventiveness," a term exemplifying the genius and innovativeness of New Zealanders, has led to remarkable experience exercises. Stream sailing, imagined by New Zealander Sir William Hamilton, represents this inventiveness.

Fly boat administrators in Queenstown and different areas move adrenaline junkies through limited waterway gulches at elating paces, executing high velocity twists and moves that exhibit the ability of these spry vessels.

Besides, New Zealand's obligation to somewhere safe norms in experience the travel industry has hardened its standing as a reliable objective for daredevils. Severe guidelines, authorizing necessities, and standard security evaluations are set up to guarantee that experience exercises are led with the greatest possible level of respect for members' prosperity. This obligation to somewhere safe upgrades the general insight for explorers as well as encourages a feeling of certainty and confidence in the nation's experience contributions.

The All Blacks, New Zealand's public rugby crew, encapsulate the nation's cutthroat and courageous soul. The haka, a customary Maori dance performed by the All Blacks before matches, represents strength and solidarity as well as an unyielding soul that rises above difficulties. This ethos pervades the more extensive culture, impacting the way to deal with experience with a blend of bravery, kinship, and a dash of the Kiwi "can-do" mentality.

New Zealand's standing as the experience capital of the world isn't bound to actual pursuits alone; it stretches out into the domain of true to life narrating. The amazing scenes of New Zealand have filled in as the scenery for various blockbuster films, generally strikingly the "The Master of the Rings" and "The Hobbit" sets of three coordinated by Sir Peter Jackson. The lavish vegetation of Hobbiton, the supernatural scenes of Mordor, and the grand pinnacles of the Foggy Mountains have become inseparable from the fantastical domains made by J.R.R. Tolkien and rejuvenated on the cinema. This realistic association further upgrades New Zealand's charm as an objective where the limits among the real world and dream obscure, welcoming swashbucklers to step into the locations of their #1 legendary stories.

New Zealand's standing as the experience capital of the world is a demonstration of the amicable union of its normal miracles, social ethos, and obligation to somewhere safe and secure. Whether jumping from transcending spans in Queenstown, investigating volcanic scenes in Tongariro, or experiencing marine monsters in Kaikoura, swashbucklers track down a different and elating jungle gym inside the islands of Aotearoa. As the Kiwi soul keeps on embracing the call of the wild, New Zealand stays a guide for those looking for the excitement of the obscure, the surge of adrenaline, and the extraordinary force of nature's magnificence — all woven into the actual texture of the experience capital of the world.

5.2 Explore activities such as bungee jumping, skydiving, and hiking in the spectacular landscapes.

Setting out on an investigation of New Zealand's experience exercises is to plunge carelessly into a reality where daredevils and nature fans unite.

The country's staggering scenes, from snow-covered tops to lavish valleys, act as the stage for heart-beating undertakings that reach from the notorious to the spectacular.

Bungee Bouncing:

New Zealand is broadly viewed as the origination of present day bungee bouncing, and the game has become inseparable from the country's bold soul. The town of Queenstown, settled on the shores of Lake Wakatipu in the midst of the transcending pinnacles of the Southern Alps, remains as the focal point of this gravity-resisting action. The Kawarau Scaffold, where the world's most memorable business bungee hop occurred in 1988, stays a notable site for those looking for an adrenaline rush.

As adrenaline junkies approach the edge of the extension, suspended high over the turquoise waters of the Kawarau Stream, they stand at the slope of a thrilling drop. The line, safely secured to their lower legs, pushes them into a controlled drop, making a heart-halting snapshot of weightlessness before the rope draws back, permitting members to bob and open up air. The crude magnificence of the crevasse and the surge of the waterway beneath enhance the power of the experience, making Kawarau Extension Bungy a quintessential experience for those trying courageous to go all in.

Queenstown doesn't stop at the Kawarau Extension; it offers other notable bungee encounters that take care of various degrees of trying. The Nevis Bungy, suspended high over the Nevis Waterway gorge, remains as one of the greatest business bungee bounces on the planet. The leap stage, got to by an exhilarating 134-meter streetcar ride, offers unmatched perspectives on the rough scenes beneath. The snapshot of drop from the Nevis Bungy isn't just a trial by fire yet additionally an extraordinary vantage point from which to see the value in the magnificence of New Zealand's immaculate wild.

Skydiving:

In the event that plunging from levels isn't sufficient, New Zealand welcomes swashbucklers to make it a stride further with the thrilling experience of skydiving. The opportunity of the skies, the surge of wind against the face, and the all encompassing perspectives on the country's different scenes make a tactile over-burden that is both empowering and lowering.

In Queenstown, Wanaka, and Taupo, skydiving devotees have the chance to take off over some of New Zealand's most dazzling settings. As the airplane rises to bewildering elevations, members plan for a pair bounce, got to an accomplished skydiving teacher. The jump from the plane starts a stunning drop, rushing towards the earth at speeds that can surpass 200 kilometers each hour. The drop is a tangible orchestra, with the adrenaline rush supplemented by the visual exhibition of lakes, mountains, and shores extending to the skyline.

Queenstown, encompassed by the snow-covered pinnacles of the Remarkables and the flawless waters of Lake Wakatipu, offers an especially captivating setting for skydiving. The ethereal display incorporates the Southern Alps, the rambling scenes of Fiordland, and the notable mountain goes that characterize the South Island's appeal. Wanaka, with its frigid lakes and snow capped landscape, gives a similarly hypnotizing material to a high-height plunge. In the mean time, Taupo on the North Island offers an alternate point of view, with perspectives on the immense Lake Taupo and the volcanic territory that portrays the district.

Skydiving isn't simply an undertaking; it's a fellowship with the skies and a festival of the endless excellence that stretches underneath. It changes the demonstration of falling into a fine art, a statement of opportunity that typifies the actual quintessence of New Zealand's courageous soul.

Climbing:

While bungee bouncing and skydiving take care of the thrill seekers, New Zealand's scenes likewise coax the individuals who look for a more grounded at this point similarly spectacular experience. Climbing, or slogging as it's known in Kiwi speech, offers a different scope of trails that breeze through lavish backwoods, rise high pinnacles, and wander along waterfront bluffs.

The Tongariro Elevated Crossing, situated in the UNESCO World Legacy recorded Tongariro Public Park, remains as one of New Zealand's most famous climbs. The path navigates a volcanic scene overwhelmed by the pinnacles of Mount Tongariro, Mount Ngauruhoe (Mount Destruction in "The Ruler of the Rings"), and Mount Ruapehu. The intersection, frequently hailed as one of the world's greatest day climbs, winds through emerald lakes, lunar-like cavities, and vistas that grandstand the crude, immaculate magnificence of New Zealand's wild.

The Fiordland Public Park, situated in the southwestern corner of the South Island, is home to the Milford Track, frequently alluded to as the "best stroll on the planet." This multi-day journey takes climbers through old rainforests, past flowing cascades, and close by unblemished lakes. The zenith of the excursion at Milford Sound, a stunning fjord encompassed by transcending precipices, is a prize that outperforms the actual effort of the trip.

In the South Island's West Coast, the Fox and Franz Josef Glacial masses offer a novel mix of climbing and cold investigation. Directed climbs onto the ice sheets permit travelers to cross the frigid scenes, explore through chasms, and witness the steadily changing types of these old ice masses. The juxtaposition of cold excellence against the scenery of New Zealand's rough landscape makes a strange and powerful climbing experience.

New Zealand's Division of Protection (DOC) deals with a broad organization of trails, taking care of explorers, everything being equal. The Abel Tasman Waterfront Track, twisting along the brilliant sea shores of the Abel Tasman Public Park, offers a beach front break where walkers can experience fur seals, local birds, and the turquoise waters of the Tasman Ocean.

The Kepler Track, situated in Fiordland, takes climbers on an excursion through beech woodlands, snow capped glades, and all encompassing ridgelines, giving a vivid involvement with the South Island's different biological systems.

The multi-day Routeburn Track, associating Fiordland and Mount Hopeful Public Parks, is one more gem in New Zealand's climbing crown. Crossing mountain ranges, elevated knolls, and thick timberlands, the track divulges scenes that reach from the glorious to the dreamlike. The feeling of achievement after arriving at the Harris Seat, the most noteworthy place of the path, is matched simply by the brotherhood fashioned among individual climbers and the submersion in the untamed magnificence of the Southern Alps.

Social and Beautiful Climbs:

New Zealand's experience stretches out past the actual test of climbing; it coordinates social and grand components to make a comprehensive investigation of the country's rich embroidery. The Te Araroa Trail, extending from

Cape Reinga at the northern tip of the North Island to Feign at the southern tip of the South Island, offers a persistent through-climb that traverses the length of Aotearoa. Navigating different scenes and going through social milestones, the Te Araroa is a journey for significant distance explorers looking for a significant association with New Zealand's normal and social legacy.

The Hauraki Rail Trail, twisting through the Coromandel Promontory and Hauraki Fields, offers an alternate speed of investigation. This grand cycling and strolling trail joins social encounters with the magnificence of the New Zealand open country. From memorable gold mining locales to rich scenes spotted with local greenery, the Hauraki Rail Trail is a demonstration of the country's obligation to practical the travel industry, offering swashbucklers a vivid excursion through both history and nature.

New Zealand's experience exercises, whether opposing gravity with a bungee bounce, quickly dropping from the sky in a pair skydive, or climbing through different scenes, share an ongoing idea — they unfurl in a background of unmatched regular excellence. The country's obligation to preservation, security, and the incorporation of Maori culture into outside encounters makes an undertaking embroidery that rises above the actual demonstration, welcoming members to interface with the land, the sky, and the actual substance of what makes New Zealand a sanctuary for searchers of both energy and tranquility. In these heart-beating exercises and tranquil journeys, New Zealand welcomes explorers to challenge their cutoff points as well as to find a more profound, more significant association with the marvels of Aotearoa.

5.3 Discuss the balance between adventure tourism and environmental conservation.

The harmony between experience the travel industry and natural protection addresses a fragile dance on the worldwide stage, and no place is this exchange more obvious than in New Zealand. The country, eminent for its flawless scenes and gutsy soul, faces the test of taking care of the requests of a steadily developing experience the travel industry while shielding the very environments that attract guests the primary spot.

Saving the Regular Jungle gym:

New Zealand's scenes are not just a scenery for experience; they are the quintessence of the experience. From the transcending pinnacles of the Southern Alps to the fjords of Fiordland, the nation's charm lies in its untainted normal magnificence. Perceiving this, preservation endeavors have become fundamental to the country's ethos. The Branch of Preservation (DOC) assumes a vital part in overseeing and safeguarding New Zealand's regular and social legacy, directing a broad organization of public stops, holds, and strolling tracks.

The sensitive biological systems of the nation, home to novel verdure, request cautious stewardship. Experience the travel industry, which incorporates exercises, for example, bungee hopping, skydiving, and climbing, brings a human component into these environments. The test lies in adjusting the longing to give exciting encounters the basic to limit the effect on the climate.

Maintainable Experience The travel industry:

One of the support points supporting the sensitive equilibrium is the idea of manageable experience the travel industry. New Zealand has taken steps to guarantee that the financial advantages got from experience the travel industry don't come at the expense of ecological debasement. Reasonable the travel industry rehearses focus on the drawn out strength of environments, limit carbon impressions, and advance capable commitment with nature.

In the experience capital of the world, Queenstown, administrators comply to severe ecological rules. Whether it's bungee leaping off the Kawarau Scaffold or skydiving above Lake Wakatipu, organizations perceive the need to work in a way that regards the climate. Squander decrease, energy productivity, and carbon offset drives are only a couple of the techniques utilized to moderate the natural effect of these high-adrenaline exercises.

Additionally, climbing trails, for example, the Tongariro Snow capped Crossing and the Milford Track, are dependent upon preservation disapproved of the executives. Guest numbers are checked, and gauges are carried out to forestall soil disintegration and safeguard delicate snow capped environments.

Hovels along these paths work considering supportability, integrating eco-accommodating plans and waste administration frameworks to leave insignificant hint of human presence.

Adjusting Access and Safeguarding:

A crucial part of the harmony is tracking down the right harmony between conceding admittance to these regular ponders and protecting them for people in the future. Experience the travel industry, by its actual nature, carries individuals into closeness with delicate conditions. Finding some kind of harmony includes carrying out measures that control guest numbers, manage exercises, and keep up with the environmental trustworthiness of these spaces.

For example, the Division of Preservation has carried out a standard framework for climbers on the Milford Track, restricting the quantity of trampers to guarantee that the track's biological systems can recover and stay strong. This sensitive dance between giving access and protecting the climate is a demonstration of New Zealand's obligation to economical the travel industry rehearses.

In the domain of experience exercises like bungee bouncing and skydiving, administrators team up with preservation organizations to lay out rules that limit aggravations to untamed life, streams, and encompassing vegetation. This advantageous connection between experience the travel industry organizations and preservation associations is significant for keeping up with the sensitive harmony between the excitement of the experience and the sacredness of the climate.

Local area Association and Instruction:

One more key component in this mind boggling balance is the association of nearby networks and the schooling of the two occupants and vacationers. Networks dwelling in or close to experience the travel industry areas of interest assume an imperative part in guaranteeing that the flood of guests doesn't think twice about respectability of their regular environmental factors. Drives that advance local area commitment, mindfulness, and a feeling of obligation add to the safeguarding of neighborhood environments.

Instructive projects for travelers, underscoring the standards of "leave no follow" and mindful the travel industry, are fundamental. This not just increases mindfulness about the ecological meaning of the areas they are investigating yet additionally cultivates a culture of regard and stewardship. Informed guests are bound to see the value in the delicacy of the biological systems they experience and do whatever it takes to limit their effect.

Alleviating Natural Dangers:

As experience the travel industry fills in fame, the potential for natural dangers increments. Moderating these dangers is a nonstop interaction that includes continuous examination, mechanical development, and versatile administration techniques.

In districts with frigid conditions, for example, the Fox and Franz Josef Glacial masses, the effects of environmental change represent a specific test. The retreat of ice sheets modifies the scene and influences the openness and well-being of experience exercises. Administrators should adjust their practices to the changing circumstances while adding to more extensive discussions about environment activity.

The Waitomo Glowworm Caverns, an interesting underground marvel, face difficulties connected with guest people strolling through and the expected interruption of fragile environments. Protection endeavors here include painstakingly oversaw visits, framework advancement that limits aggravation, and continuous exploration to figure out the caverns' natural elements.

Administrative Systems and Requirement:

To keep up with the sensitive harmony between experience the travel industry and natural protection, vigorous administrative systems are pivotal. Government bodies, for example, the Division of Protection, work pair with neighborhood specialists to lay out and authorize guidelines that administer the activity of experience the travel industry exercises.

The administrative structures cover a range of contemplations, including ecological effect evaluations, wellbeing norms, and adherence to manageability rules. Customary reviews and examinations guarantee that administrators agree with these principles and face ramifications for infringement. This administrative oversight is an indispensable part of safeguarding the trustworthiness of New Zealand's normal jungle gym.

Difficulties and Future Contemplations:
While New Zealand has taken estimable steps in accomplishing a harmony between experience the travel industry and natural protection, challenges continue, and future contemplations are vital. The rising prominence of specific exercises and objections requires a proactive way to deal with overseeing guest numbers and forestalling abuse of delicate regions.

Environmental change represents an overall danger to a considerable lot of New Zealand's normal attractions. Frigid retreat, changed atmospheric conditions, and moving biological systems all effect the scenes that act as the material for experience the travel industry. Adjusting to these progressions and executing techniques for environment versatility become fundamental in protecting the very conditions that make New Zealand an undertaking sanctuary.

Innovative headways, for example, the utilization of electric-controlled vessels for water-based exercises and the advancement of eco-accommodating experience gear, add to limiting the carbon impression related with experience the travel industry. Putting resources into imaginative arrangements that line up with manageable practices guarantees that the business can keep on flourishing without compromising the climate.

The continuous exchange between experience the travel industry partners, preservationists, neighborhood networks, and government bodies is fundamental for exploring the developing scene of experience the travel industry mindfully. Cooperative endeavors can distinguish arising difficulties, refine best practices, and encourage a common obligation to saving the exceptional regular legacy that characterizes New Zealand.

The entwining of experience the travel industry and natural protection in New Zealand epitomizes an agreeable relationship that, while multifaceted, is fundamental for the country's reasonable turn of events. The country's obligation to shielding its normal jungle gym while offering exciting encounters is a demonstration of its ground breaking approach.

Through reasonable the travel industry rehearses, local area contribution, training drives, and administrative systems, New Zealand has laid out a model that adjusts the monetary advantages of experience the travel industry with the basic to safeguard its environmental fortunes. The sensitive dance between the daredevils and the conditions they investigate highlights a promise to a future where experience and preservation coincide, guaranteeing that the normal marvels of Aotearoa proceed to spellbind and motivate ages to come.

CHAPTER 6

"Kiwi Hospitality"

Kiwi Friendliness: A Warm Hug in Aotearoa

In the core of the South Pacific, where lavish scenes and charming shorelines join, there exists a country with a standing that stretches out a long ways past its stunning view. New Zealand, or Aotearoa in the native Maori language, isn't just famous for its regular ponders yet in addition celebrated for the glow and earnestness of its kin. At the center of this extraordinary social character is "Kiwi cordiality," a term that typifies the veritable benevolence, transparency, and inviting soul for which New Zealanders, tenderly known as Kiwis, are globally perceived.

The Pith of Kiwi Accommodation:

Kiwi neighborliness isn't simply a bunch of endorsed activities or prearranged signals; it is a profoundly imbued part of New Zealand's social texture. At its pith, Kiwi neighborliness mirrors a real longing to cause guests to feel appreciated, however embraced as a component of the local area. It goes past the conditional idea of administration and the travel industry, reaching out into a domain where connections are instilled with a veritable feeling of care and thought.

From the second one goes to the shores of Aotearoa, the soul of Kiwi accommodation becomes unmistakable. Whether showing up at a clamoring global air terminal or investigating a curious provincial town, the receptiveness of individuals is clear. Outsiders are welcomed with a warm "Kia ora," a Maori articulation meaning both "hi" and "be well," mirroring a social affirmation of the prosperity and positive cooperations with others.

Social Foundations of Kiwi Neighborliness:

To really comprehend Kiwi neighborliness, one should dig into the social roots that shape this one of a kind part of New Zealand's personality. The Maori public, the native Polynesian occupants of Aotearoa, have a rich custom of manaakitanga, an idea that typifies the soul of liberality, cordiality, and care for other people. Manaakitanga mirrors a significant comprehension that the prosperity of the local area is interconnected with the prosperity of every person.

In Maori culture, the idea of whanaungatanga, or family relationship, further upgrades the feeling of connectedness. Guests to New Zealand are frequently treated not as visitors but rather as whanau, or relatives, establishing a climate where the lines among local people and guests obscure. This social ethos is a main impetus behind the glow that characterizes Kiwi neighborliness — a glow that rises above social limits and impacts anybody sufficiently lucky to encounter it.

Friendliness in Ordinary Connections:

Kiwi friendliness isn't bound to formal settings or arranged occasions; it is woven into the embroidered artwork of regular daily existence. Whether walking around an energetic ranchers' market, drawing in with local people at a local bar, or looking for headings from a bystander, each cooperation turns into a chance to encounter the genuine benevolence that portrays New Zealanders.

In little provincial towns and clamoring metropolitan focuses the same, Kiwis show a veritable interest in others. The idea of "taking the time" is a sign of Kiwi neighborliness, where people are not hurried however participated in slow discussions. This sluggish speed mirrors a social comprehension that connections are esteemed over proficiency, and snapshots of association are loved.

Facilities: Where Friendliness Sees as a Home:

The exemplification of Kiwi cordiality frequently finds its most packed articulation in the facilities dissipated across the islands of Aotearoa. From enchanting overnight boardinghouses to lavish cabins, each stay turns into a part in the story of neighborliness.

In numerous facilities, has are owners as well as narrators, anxious to share stories of neighborhood legend, suggest unlikely treasures, and give bits of knowledge that guide guests through a real Kiwi experience. The possibility of visitors as brief individuals from the more distant family penetrates the feel, making an environment where the limits among host and guest are liquid.

A quintessential Kiwi experience is viewed as in the "bach" culture. Articulated "cluster," these occasion homes, frequently settled in waterfront or provincial settings, encapsulate the laid-back appeal of New Zealand accommodation. Guests who decide to remain in a bach are invited into a residence as well as into a lifestyle — one that energizes unwinding, association with nature, and the basic delight of being encircled by excellence.

Sharing the Abundance: Culinary Neighborliness:

The Kiwi way to deal with neighborliness stretches out to the culinary domain, where a real energy for new, nearby fixings and innovative culinary articulations becomes the dominant focal point. In bistros, eateries, and, surprisingly, nearby homes, food turns into a vehicle for sharing flavors as well as the embodiment of Kiwi culture.

The idea of a "Kiwi grill" is famous — a get-together where loved ones combine around a barbecue, relishing the smoky smells of sizzling meats and vegetables. A mutual encounter rises above the demonstration of eating, typifying the sociability and comprehensiveness inborn in Kiwi cordiality.

Ranch to-table practices are profoundly implanted in New Zealand's culinary scene, with ranchers' business sectors offering a dynamic feature of privately obtained produce, distinctive items, and hand crafted delights. The association between the land and the plate isn't simply a pattern however an impression of a social obligation to maintainability and an appreciation for the lavishness of New Zealand's farming abundance.

Maori Welcome: The Powhiri:

For some guests to New Zealand, the quintessential articulation of Kiwi neighborliness is the powhiri, a conventional Maori invite function. Whether directed at a marae (a collective gathering ground) or integrated into formal occasions, the powhiri is an emblematic hug that reaches out to visitors the most noteworthy type of regard.

The powhiri unfurls with a progression of ceremonies, each loaded down with social importance. The test, or wero, is a motion that tests the expectations of guests, representing both verifiable carefulness and the longing for quiet communication. The trading of talks, or whaikorero, permits the two hosts and visitors to communicate feelings of appreciated, appreciation, and association. The squeezing of noses, or hongi, is an actual indication of the blending of breath, representing the sharing of life and soul.

Taking part in a powhiri isn't just a formal demonstration; a vivid encounter welcomes people into the core of Maori culture. The credibility of the gladly received, combined with the common customs, makes a significant feeling of having a place — a sign of Kiwi friendliness that reaches out a long ways past the term of the actual service.

Kiwi Humor: A Neighborliness Sidekick:

Vital to the scene of Kiwi cordiality is the prestigious Kiwi comical inclination — a magnificent mix of mind, humility, and a hint of disrespectfulness. Humor turns into a sidekick in cordiality, a method for separating boundaries, encouraging association, and making a cheerful climate.

Whether participating in chat with local people at a bar, standing by listening to a local escort's tales, or just imparting a snicker to recently discovered companions, the Kiwi funny bone is a widespread language that rises above social contrasts. It is an encouragement to partake in the delight existing apart from everything else, to see the value in life's peculiarities, and to explore the exciting bends in the road of the excursion cheerfully.

Challenges and Developing Elements:

While Kiwi cordiality is a loved part of New Zealand's character, it isn't invulnerable to the difficulties of a quickly influencing world. The rising flood of worldwide guests, combined with the effect of worldwide occasions, requires a continuous assessment of how accommodation is broadened and experienced.

The travel industry pressures on well known objections bring up issues about supportability, protection, and the conservation of neighborhood societies. Finding some kind of harmony between inviting guests and protecting the regular and social fortunes that characterize Kiwi neighborliness turns into a complicated undertaking. Networks, as a team with specialists, are confronted with the undertaking of dealing with the developing elements of the travel industry to guarantee that the quintessence of friendliness stays real and manageable.

6.1 Explore the warm and welcoming nature of the Kiwi people.

Investigating the Warm and Inviting Nature of the Kiwi Public: An Excursion into Kiwi Friendliness

New Zealand, settled in the southwestern Pacific Sea, isn't just eminent for its shocking scenes yet in addition celebrated for the glow and cordiality of its kin — the Kiwis. Past the stunning view of rich mountains, flawless lakes, and brilliant sea shores, it is the certified and inviting nature of the Kiwi nation that has an enduring effect on guests. This glow, frequently alluded to as "Kiwi neighborliness," is a social trademark well established in the practices, values, and certifiable benevolence of the country's occupants.

Social Groundworks of Kiwi Friendliness:

At the core of Kiwi friendliness lies a rich social embroidery woven by the native Maori individuals and later enhanced by rushes of European pilgrims. The Maori idea of manaakitanga, meaning friendliness and care for other people, fills in as a primary rule molding the Kiwi way to deal with inviting visitors. It typifies a profound feeling of regard, liberality, and an eagerness to impart the magnificence of Aotearoa to the individuals who step onto its shores.

In Maori culture, connections are foremost, and the idea of whanaungatanga, or family relationship, builds up the possibility that guests are visitors as well as individuals from a more distant family. This social ethos stretches out past the native networks, pervading the more extensive society and impacting the manner in which Kiwis cooperate with individuals from varying backgrounds.

The Hello: Kia Ora and Then some:

The hello in New Zealand is in excess of a basic welcome; it is an impression of the Kiwi obligation to warmth and neighborliness. "Kia ora," a Maori expression meaning both "hi" and "be well," is the most widely recognized method for inviting somebody in New Zealand. It conveys with it a certified wish for the prosperity of the individual, establishing the vibe for positive and deferential collaborations.

The glow of the hello stretches out indeed to include motions, for example, the hongi — a conventional Maori nose press and trade of breath representing solidarity and association. While not an everyday practice, the hongi is much of the time seen during formal events, adding an extraordinary touch to stylized invites and fashioning a more profound feeling of connection.

Ordinary Associations: Where Neighborliness Sparkles:

The genuine substance of Kiwi accommodation uncovers itself in regular cooperations. Whether in clamoring metropolitan focuses or far off provincial networks, Kiwis are known for their congeniality, cordiality, and veritable interest in others. The laid-back and genuine nature of New Zealanders establishes a climate where outsiders are not just endured yet heartily embraced.

In unassuming communities, local people frequently carve out opportunity to take part in relaxed discussions with guests, sharing experiences about the nearby culture, suggesting unlikely treasures, and making an environment of brotherhood. This sluggish speed of life, an impression of the Kiwi ethos, energizes significant associations that go past surface cooperations.

Facilities: Where Visitors Become Whanau:

The encapsulation of Kiwi neighborliness frequently finds its most packed articulation in the facilities dissipated across the islands of Aotearoa. From comfortable overnight boardinghouses to lavish cabins, each stay turns into a chance for guests to encounter the glow and truthfulness of Kiwi has.

Dissimilar to the customs of customary neighborliness, Kiwi has frequently exceed everyone's expectations to cause visitors to feel like piece of the family. From sharing home-prepared feasts to giving customized suggestions to investigation, has endeavor to establish a climate where guests don't simply have a spot to remain yet feel really invited.

The casual and authentic collaborations reach out past the walls of facilities. Guests remaining in Kiwi homes, whether through homestays or occasion rentals, frequently end up submerged in the neighborhood lifestyle. The Kiwi practice of opening one's home to visitors mirrors a feeling of comprehensiveness and a longing to share the excellence of the country on an individual level.

Culinary Encounters: A Sample of Kiwi Cordiality:

Culinary experiences in New Zealand are about the flavors as well as the glow with which dinners are shared. The Kiwi neighborliness stretches out to the feasting table, where sharing a dinner turns into a mutual encounter, cultivating associations and making enduring recollections.

The quintessential Kiwi grill, usually known as a "barbie," is in excess of a culinary occasion; it is a party where loved ones meet up around a barbecue. The demonstration of cooking outside and sharing a feast under the open sky typifies the loose and jovial nature of Kiwi friendliness.

In bistros, cafés, and, surprisingly, neighborhood homes, the Kiwi enthusiasm for new, nearby fixings and imaginative culinary articulations is discernible. Guests frequently find themselves enjoying heavenly feasts as well as participating in discussions with gourmet experts and local people, making an all encompassing and vivid culinary experience.

Social Customs: Powhiri and Then some:

A huge articulation of Kiwi neighborliness is found in the customary Maori invite function known as the powhiri. Whether directed at a marae (a common gathering ground) or integrated into formal occasions, the powhiri is a representative hug that expands the most elevated type of regard to visitors.

The powhiri unfurls with ceremonial accuracy, every component conveying social importance. The test (wero) tests the goals of guests, the discourses (whaikorero) permit the two hosts and visitors to communicate opinions of welcome, and the squeezing of noses (hongi) represents the sharing of breath and life. Taking part in a powhiri is certainly not a detached demonstration yet an encouragement to draw in with Maori culture in a significant and vivid manner.

Past the powhiri, Kiwi social practices frequently include music, dance, and narrating. Guests might wind up invited into a local area with a haka, a customary Maori dance that implies strength, solidarity, and a strong articulation of welcome. These social practices make a feeling of association and inclusivity, permitting guests to encounter the core of Kiwi neighborliness.

The Kiwi Funny bone: A Common Chuckling:

Vital to the scene of Kiwi friendliness is the famous Kiwi funny bone — a magnificent mix of mind, humility, and a dash of flippancy. Humor turns into a buddy in cordiality, a method for separating boundaries, cultivating association, and making a happy climate.

Whether participating in chitchat with local people at a bar, standing by listening to a local area expert's tales, or just imparting a chuckle to newly discovered companions, the Kiwi funny bone is a widespread language that rises above social contrasts. It is a challenge to partake in the delight existing apart from everything else, to see the value in life's characteristics, and to explore the exciting bends in the road of the excursion happily.

Difficulties and Eventual fate of Kiwi Cordiality:

While Kiwi cordiality is an esteemed part of New Zealand's personality, it isn't without its difficulties, especially in that frame of mind of a quickly impacting world and a developing the travel industry. The rising flood of worldwide guests, combined with the effect of worldwide occasions, requires a smart way to deal with safeguarding the validness and manageability of Kiwi neighborliness.

The travel industry pressures on famous objections bring up issues about the limit of networks to deal with the inundation of guests while keeping up with the nature of the visitor experience. Finding some kind of harmony between inviting visitors and protecting the normal and social fortunes that characterize Kiwi friendliness turns into a perplexing undertaking.

Networks, in a joint effort with specialists, are confronted with the undertaking of dealing with the developing elements of the travel industry to guarantee that the quintessence of neighborliness stays real and economical. This incorporates resolving issues like over-the travel industry, protection, and the safeguarding of nearby societies.

The fate of Kiwi neighborliness lies in a fragile harmony between embracing the monetary advantages of the travel industry and defending the legitimacy that makes New Zealand a sought-after objective. Reasonable the travel industry rehearses, local area contribution, and mindful guest conduct are critical parts in guaranteeing that Kiwi friendliness keeps on flourishing without compromising the very esteems that characterize it.

6.2 Discuss the importance of hospitality in New Zealand culture.

The Substance of Friendliness in New Zealand Culture: A More profound Investigation

In the charming domain of Aotearoa, referred to the world as New Zealand, neighborliness isn't just a social practice — it is a lifestyle profoundly implanted in the texture of the country. Past the tremendous scenes and normal ponders that characterize the country, the glow, benevolence, and veritable inviting soul of the Kiwi public contribute fundamentally to the one of a kind appeal of New Zealand.

In this investigation, we dive into the significant significance of cordiality in New Zealand culture, grasping its underlying foundations, appearances, and its advancing job in forming the country's personality.

Social Underpinnings of Kiwi Friendliness:

To grasp the meaning of friendliness in New Zealand, one must initially follow its foundations to the native Maori culture. Key to the Maori lifestyle is the idea of manaakitanga, a term epitomizing the act of friendliness and care for other people. Manaakitanga goes past simple graciousness; it exemplifies a profound regard for the prosperity of others, cultivating a feeling of having a place and interconnectedness.

In Maori custom, visitors are thought of as holy, and the demonstration of inviting them is a sacrosanct obligation. The standards of manaakitanga reach out past the native networks, pervading the more extensive New Zealand society. Kiwis, as individuals of New Zealand are warmly known, have embraced and coordinated these social qualities, making a public character where friendliness isn't simply a motion however an essential part of connections.

The Hello: A Kia Ora Welcome:

The declaration of neighborliness in New Zealand frequently starts with a basic yet significant hello: "Kia ora." This Maori expression, meaning both "hi" and "be well," establishes the vibe for cooperations by not just recognizing the presence of the other individual yet in addition communicating a certifiable wish for their prosperity. It embodies the Kiwi obligation to establishing a climate where people feel saw as well as focused on.

This warm hello is in excess of a semantic show; a social practice mirrors the Kiwi ethos of benevolence and transparency. Whether traded between companions, colleagues, or outsiders, the expression of "Kia ora" conveys the heaviness of social custom, welcoming people to interface on a level that rises above the outer layer of everyday trades.

Social Inclusivity and Whanaungatanga:

At the core of Kiwi accommodation lies the idea of whanaungatanga, which means connection or family association. This social rule underscores the significance of connections and interconnectedness. Guests to New Zealand are not treated as outcasts; all things considered, they are invited into a feeling of local area and familial bonds.

In the soul of whanaungatanga, visitors are viewed as transitory individuals from the more distant family, or whanau. This comprehensive outlook cultivates a climate where people from different foundations feel a feeling of having a place, separating the obstructions of social contrasts. The Kiwi obligation to whanaungatanga stretches out to networks, work environments, and get-togethers, making a public ethos that values associations and connections.

Regular Cooperations: The Unfurling of Kiwi Warmth:

Kiwi friendliness isn't saved for formal events or exceptional occasions; it is woven into the texture of day to day existence. In both metropolitan habitats and provincial networks, New Zealanders are known for their congeniality, amicability, and readiness to take part in authentic discussions.

The laid-back and unassuming nature of Kiwis adds to a climate where outsiders are not seen with doubt but rather welcomed with interest and transparency. Whether in a nearby bistro, a local market, or a local area occasion, guests frequently wind up participated in relaxed discussions, sharing stories, and shaping associations that go past the transient idea of the travel industry.

This sluggish way to deal with life is intelligent of the Kiwi reasoning that esteems the nature of connections over the amount. The significance put on carving out opportunity to interface with others, independent of their experience, highlights the social obligation to encouraging connections and making a general public where friendliness is a resided insight.

Facilities: From Hosts to Whanau:

The sign of Kiwi friendliness turns out to be especially articulated in the domain of facilities. From curious overnight boardinghouses to extravagant cabins, the experience of remaining in New Zealand isn't just about the conveniences; it is about the glow and truthfulness of the hosts.

Dissimilar to the conditional idea of numerous accommodation enterprises, Kiwi has frequently go past the normal standards to cause visitors to feel like piece of the family. This casual and individual touch establishes a climate where guests don't simply track down a spot to remain yet experience a certified feeling of having a place.

The possibility of visitors becoming impermanent individuals from the whanau isn't restricted to formal facilities. Occasion rentals, ranch stays, and, surprisingly, the famous Kiwi bach (occasion home) offer guests a chance to drench themselves in the Kiwi lifestyle. Sharing feasts, stories, and encounters with has changes the stay into a social trade, permitting visitors to acquire bits of knowledge into the neighborhood lifestyle.

Culinary Practices: Sharing a Sample of Aotearoa:

Kiwi cordiality stretches out to the culinary domain, where sharing a feast turns into a hallowed demonstration of association. The idea of eating together isn't simply a routine yet a festival of connections and shared encounters.

The Kiwi grill, conversationally known as a "barbie," is a notorious articulation of this culinary neighborliness. Loved ones gathering around a barbecue, enjoying the kinds of privately obtained meats and vegetables, typify the loose and friendly nature of Kiwi life. It isn't just about the food; it is tied in with making an air of fellowship and shared delight.

Ranch to-table practices are profoundly imbued in New Zealand's culinary scene. Ranchers' business sectors, where local people and guests the same can investigate new produce and distinctive items, typify the obligation to reasonable and privately obtained fixings. Culinary encounters in New Zealand go past the sense of taste; they become an excursion into the social subtleties and values that characterize Kiwi cordiality.

Social Practices: The Powhiri and Then some:

One of the most significant articulations of Kiwi accommodation is found in the customary Maori invite function — the powhiri. Whether directed at a marae or integrated into formal occasions, the powhiri is a stylized hug that broadens the most noteworthy type of regard to visitors.

The powhiri is a carefully arranged succession of customs, each weighed down with social importance. The test (wero) represents both authentic attentiveness and the craving for serene connection. Addresses (whaikorero) permit hosts and visitors to communicate feelings of appreciated and association. The squeezing of noses (hongi) is an actual sign of shared breath, representing solidarity and common regard.

Taking part in a powhiri is definitely not a detached demonstration; a vivid encounter welcomes people into the core of Maori culture. The genuineness of the gladly received, combined with the common customs, makes a significant feeling of having a place — a sign of Kiwi neighborliness that reaches out a long ways past the term of the actual service.

The Kiwi Funny bone: A Social Buddy:

Indispensable to the scene of Kiwi neighborliness is the prestigious Kiwi comical inclination. Clever, humble, and implanted with a hint of disrespectfulness, the Kiwi funny bone turns into a social sidekick in cordiality. It isn't simply a type of diversion; it is a method for separating hindrances, encouraging association, and making a carefree climate.

Whether participating in exchange with local people at a bar, standing by listening to a local escort's stories, or basically imparting a snicker to newly discovered companions, the Kiwi funny bone rises above social contrasts. It fills in as a widespread language that welcomes all, paying little mind to foundation, to partake in the delight existing apart from everything else.

Difficulties and Future Elements: Adjusting Development and Genuineness:

While Kiwi neighborliness is profoundly esteemed, it isn't insusceptible to the difficulties presented by a quickly influencing world and the effects of a developing the travel industry. The rising flood of worldwide guests, combined with the results of worldwide occasions, requires an insightful way to deal with keeping up with the validness of Kiwi neighborliness.

The travel industry pressures on famous objections bring up issues about the limit of networks to deal with the inundation of guests while saving the nature of the visitor experience. The fragile harmony between monetary advantages and the safeguarding of normal and social fortunes turns into a perplexing undertaking.

Systems for manageable the travel industry rehearses, local area association, and dependable guest conduct are critical in guaranteeing that Kiwi cordiality stays certifiable and reasonable. The difficulties of over-the travel industry, protection, and the conservation of nearby societies require a cooperative exertion from networks, specialists, and the travel industry to explore the developing elements.

6.3 Share stories of travelers' experiences and connections with locals.

Investigating Aotearoa Through Voyagers' Stories: Bonds Produced in Kiwi Neighborliness

New Zealand, with its enthralling scenes and kind local people, offers something other than an objective; it gives a vivid embroidery of encounters woven through associations with the Kiwi public. As voyagers set out on ventures across the North and South Islands, their accounts unfurl with a consistent idea — the veritable cordiality and significant associations imparted to local people. In this investigation, we dive into the stories of voyagers whose encounters rise above the conventional, uncovering the profundity of associations fashioned in the hug of Kiwi accommodation.

A Warm Invite in Wellington:

Sophie, an energetic voyager from France, describes her appearance in Wellington, the lively capital settled at the southern tip of the North Island. Anxious to investigate the city's social contributions, she ended up at a neighborhood bistro, tasting on a level white — the notable Kiwi espresso. As she wondered about the barista's expertise, a well disposed neighborhood named Emma started up a discussion.

Emma, detecting Sophie's interest, shared bits of knowledge into Wellington's specialty scene as well as stretched out a solicitation to a local area craftsmanship occasion soon thereafter. Fascinated, Sophie joined Emma and her companions, drenching herself in the nearby workmanship local area. The night unfurled as a festival of imagination, culture, and newly discovered kinships, exemplifying the soul of Kiwi friendliness that goes past surface collaborations.

A Seaside Association in Coromandel:

Mark, a nature devotee from Canada, tried to investigate the perfect excellence of the Coromandel Promontory. His process drove him to a seaside town where he found an unlikely treasure — a family-run quaint little inn neglecting the turquoise waters.

The hosts, Jane and Richard, invited him with veritable warmth, causing him to feel like piece of their more distant family.

Every morning, Imprint got up to the fragrance of a hand crafted Kiwi breakfast, and nights were spent assembled around the chimney, sharing stories. Jane and Richard, enthusiastic about their area, turned into Imprint's aides, driving him to disconnected sea shores, lavish woods, and neighborhood areas of interest known exclusively to the occupants. The association framed in those days rose above the job of hosts and visitor, developing into an enduring bond established in shared encounters and an affection for the waterfront safe house.

Social Drenching in Rotorua:

Alex, a brave explorer from the US, tried to dive into Maori culture in Rotorua. His process drove him to a Maori town where he was invited with a conventional powhiri. The people group's hug went past the stately ceremonies; Alex ended up took part in discussions with neighborhood older folks, finding out about their traditions, legends, and the meaning of the land.

As the night unfurled with a conventional hangi feast, Alex felt a significant feeling of association. The musical beats of the haka, the common giggling, and the accommodation stretched out by the Maori people group made a permanent imprint. In the days that followed, Alex was welcome to take part in ordinary exercises, from winding around meetings to local meetings. The submersion into Maori life turned into a groundbreaking encounter, featuring the force of neighborliness in cultivating multifaceted comprehension.

Backwoods Holding in Fiordland:

For Lara, a brave climber from Germany, the charm of Fiordland's rough scenes called her to investigate its boondocks trails. Wandering into the wild, she experienced a gathering of Kiwi trampers (climbers) drove by Tom, a carefully prepared guide with a profound love for the land. Which began as a common path turned into an excursion of kinship and shared appreciation for the untamed excellence encompassing them.

In the nights, by the sparkle of an open air fire, the gathering traded stories — of undertakings, challenges, and the basic delights of being submerged in nature. Tom, in obvious Kiwi design, not just shared his insight into the vegetation yet in addition imparted in the gathering a feeling of obligation toward safeguarding the wild. As they explored the Fiordland trails together, the bonds shaped rose above the transient idea of the excursion, exemplifying the ethos of Kiwi friendliness in the core of the wild.

The Bach Involvement with Abel Tasman:

Abel Tasman Public Park, with its brilliant sea shores and turquoise waters, turned into the scenery for Maria's Kiwi experience. Settling on a bach stay — a notable New Zealand occasion home — Maria wound up in the curious beach front town of Kaiteriteri. Her hosts, Dave and Sarah, invited her into their bach as well as into their local area.

Days were spent investigating stowed away inlets and kayaking along the shoreline. Nights unfurled with shared dinners and stargazing from the bach's deck. Dave and Sarah, epitomizing the soul of Kiwi accommodation, shared stories of the town's set of experiences and acquainted Maria with the neighborhood customs. The bach experience turned out to be something other than a spot to remain; it turned into a gateway to neighborhood life and a getting through association with the seaside local area.

From Metropolitan Investigations to Country Retreats:

As these accounts unfurl, a consistent idea arises — the different settings where associations with local people are manufactured. Whether in the metropolitan buzz of Wellington or the serene scenes of Coromandel, the profundity of Kiwi friendliness stays steady. From social submersions in Rotorua to boondocks holding in Fiordland, the soul of association rises above geological limits. Indeed, even the curious bach in Abel Tasman turns into a door to both normal miracles and local area ties.

These stories likewise exhibit the flexibility of Kiwi cordiality, reaching out from metropolitan experiences to rustic retreats. Whether in the core of a city or the isolation of the boondocks, voyagers end up embraced by the receptiveness, cordiality, and certified care of the Kiwi public. It is this dynamic and comprehensive nature of neighborliness that leaves a getting through influence on the individuals who navigate the assorted scenes of Aotearoa.

The Job of Kiwi Cordiality in Forming Encounters:

What recognizes these encounters isn't just the amazing landscape or the experience looking for soul of the explorers; it is the urgent pretended by Kiwi cordiality in molding their excursions. Local people, going about as more than guides or has, become channels to the spirit of New Zealand. They share the actual scenes as well as the social lavishness, the practices, and the narratives that make Aotearoa one of a kind.

Kiwi friendliness isn't restricted to prearranged associations; it is a natural, living power that changes experiences into associations. The tales of Emma in Wellington, Jane and Richard in Coromandel, the Maori people group in Rotorua, Tom in Fiordland, and Dave and Sarah in Abel Tasman epitomize this extraordinary influence. What starts as an explorer looking for encounters develops into a common investigation, a social trade, and frequently, a long lasting bond.

The Far reaching influence of Veritable Associations:

These accounts additionally delineate the gradually expanding influence of certified associations. As voyagers structure bonds with local people, they become spectators as well as members in the social story of New Zealand. The effect goes past the term of their visit, impacting the points of view they convey home and, at times, motivating a re-visitation of the shores of Aotearoa.

Sophie, having encountered the glow of Wellington's craft local area, proceeded with her excursion with a recently discovered appreciation for the force of nearby associations. Mark, charmed by the seaside asylum of Coromandel, left with more than pleasant recollections; he conveyed with him the soul of neighborliness that characterized his visit. Alex, contacted by the drenching into Maori culture, turned into a representative of understanding and social trade.

These accounts highlight the getting through nature of associations produced in the hug of Kiwi cordiality. The effect reverberates in the recollections of explorers as well as in the accounts they share with companions, family, and individual globe-trotters. It turns into a demonstration of the groundbreaking force of movement when directed by the legitimacy of human associations.

Challenges and Developing Elements:

While these stories portray agreeable associations, recognizing the difficulties and advancing elements in the domain of movement and hospitality is fundamental. The rising prominence of New Zealand as an objective carries with it the intricacies of overseeing the travel industry pressures, protecting neighborhood societies, and guaranteeing the maintainability of normal marvels.

Networks, similar to those experienced by explorers, end up at the convergence of neighborliness and the requirement for dependable the travel industry rehearses. Adjusting the convergence of guests with the protection of the climate and the credibility of nearby encounters turns into a sensitive undertaking. The test lies in cultivating a cooperative relationship where voyagers contribute emphatically to the spots they investigate, leaving a positive effect on both the climate and the networks.

CHAPTER 7

"Culinary Delights"

Culinary Pleasures of Aotearoa: A Gastronomic Excursion through New Zealand's Rich Flavors

Setting out on a culinary excursion through New Zealand, or Aotearoa as it is lovingly known, is to dig into an existence where unblemished scenes are reflected in the newness and variety of its food. From the fruitful fields to the plentiful oceans, New Zealand's culinary scene mirrors a concordance among custom and development, all while praising the remarkable kinds of the land. In this investigation, we adventure into the rich embroidery of Aotearoa's culinary joys, where each dish recounts a story, and each chomp is a festival of the country's normal abundance.

The Substance of Kiwi Food:

New Zealand's culinary character is an impression of its geological variety, mixing native Maori customs with European impacts and a cutting edge Pacific Edge pizazz. The substance of Kiwi food lies in its obligation to new, occasional, and privately obtained fixings, permitting the regular flavors to become the dominant focal point. From the prolific fields of Waikato to the fish rich waters of the Marlborough Sounds, the culinary excursion unfurls with an ensemble of tastes that reflect the country's different scenes.

Ranch to-Table Customs:

The core of New Zealand's culinary experience lies in its homestead to-table practices, where the excursion from field to plate is a demonstration of maintainability and quality. Voyagers frequently wind up in beguiling country bistros, encompassed by moving slopes and farmlands, enjoying dishes created from fixings obtained just past the kitchen entryway.

In the Waikato area, eminent for its rich fields, dairy ranches produce a portion of the world's best cheeses. A visit to a nearby dairy ranch not just offers a brief look into the cheddar making process yet in addition welcomes tastings of smooth blue cheeses and flavorful goudas, matched with distinctive saltines and privately created wines. The obligation to economical cultivating rehearses guarantees that each chomp recounts an account of the land and the hands that develop it.

Kai Moana - Abundance from the Oceans:

As an island country encompassed by the tremendous Pacific Sea, New Zealand brags an abundance fish that becomes the dominant focal point in its culinary collection. The Maori expression "kai moana" means "food from the ocean," and it embodies the veneration for the sea's contributions. From the fragile Feign shellfish to the delicious green-lipped mussels of Marlborough, the fish insight in Aotearoa is a demonstration of the country's beach front overflow.

In the beach front town of Kaikoura, a fish sanctuary on the South Island, explorers can enjoy a gala of crawfish, paua (abalone), and blue cod — all obtained from the flawless waters simply seaward. The accentuation on reasonable fishing rehearses guarantees that the culinary joys are scrumptious as well as lined up with the standards of capable stewardship of the marine climate.

Hangi - Maori Earth Broiler Custom:

To really comprehend the profundity of Kiwi food is to participate in the Maori custom of hangi. This extremely old cooking strategy includes slow-preparing food in an earth broiler, outfitting the normal intensity from warmed rocks covered in the earth. The outcome is an interesting and tasty culinary experience that honors both the Maori legacy and the abundance of Aotearoa's territory.

In Rotorua, a city known for its geothermal action, guests can observer the complicated course of setting up a hangi. The hearty smell of slow-cooked meats, vegetables, and sweet treats consumes the space as the food is uncovered, uncovering a delicious and smoky blowout that catches the substance of Maori cordiality.

Pavlova - A Sweet Ensemble:

No investigation of Kiwi cooking is finished without enjoying a cut of pavlova — a pastry that has become inseparable from New Zealand and Australia. This meringue-based treat, enhanced with new foods grown from the ground cream, is a brilliant finale to numerous Kiwi feasts. The pavlova's light and breezy surface, combined with the explosion of flavors from occasional natural products, embody the pleasantness of New Zealand's culinary contributions.

The beginning of pavlova is a wellspring of cordial discussion between New Zealand and Australia, yet its ubiquity in Kiwi families and bistros is unquestionable. Whether delighted in a clamoring metropolitan bistro in Auckland or a comfortable shoreline restaurant in Dunedin, pavlova addresses the amicable combination of nearby fixings and global impacts that characterize the country's culinary scene.

High quality Wines - A Toast to Terroir:

New Zealand's obligation to greatness in winemaking deserves it a put on the worldwide stage, with its Sauvignon Blancs, Pinot Noirs, and different varietals acquiring global praise. The country's special terroir, portrayed by different microclimates and fruitful soil, grants particular qualities to its wines, making each taste a declaration of Aotearoa's normal abundance.

In the Marlborough locale, prestigious for its Sauvignon Blanc, voyagers can investigate grape plantations that stretch across moving slopes and valleys. Tasting rooms offer a tangible excursion through fresh whites and exquisite reds, frequently joined by clearing perspectives on the plant covered scenes. The blossoming wine the travel industry commends the craft of winemaking as well as furnishes a chance to interface with the vintners and gain experiences into the enthusiasm that goes into each jug.

Kumara - Maori Yam Pleasure:

The humble kumara, or yam, holds an extraordinary spot in both Maori and Kiwi cooking. With its lively orange tissue and sweet, nutty flavor, kumara includes noticeably in different dishes, from customary hangi to contemporary culinary manifestations. Its flexibility and dietary benefit make it a darling fixing that typifies the soul of New Zealand's gastronomic variety.

In the Hawke's Straight district, where prolific soils and a warm environment make ideal circumstances for kumara development, explorers can relish dishes that grandstand the yam's reach. Whether simmered, crushed, or integrated into creative treats, kumara mirrors the culinary resourcefulness that characterizes Kiwi cooking.

Buzzy Honey bee Honey - A Fluid Gold Encounter:

New Zealand's immaculate scenes not just add to the extravagance of its food yet in addition give a safe house to different widely varied vegetation.

This biodiversity is reflected in the country's special honeys, with the manuka honey standing apart as an image of New Zealand's normal riches. The excursion from hive to jostle offers a captivating look into the universe of bee-keeping and the perplexing system that changes nectar into fluid gold.

In the Narrows of Bounty, guests can investigate honey ranches where bee-keepers, clad in defensive stuff, tend to hives settled in the midst of local shrubbery. The directed visits demystify the craft of beekeeping as well as permit visitors to taste a variety of honey assortments, each with its unmistak-able flavor profile. The restorative properties credited to manuka honey add an additional layer of charm to this fluid gold, making it a sought-after gift for guests.

Present day Kiwi Combination - Culinary Development:

While customary flavors hold a unique spot, New Zealand's culinary scene likewise embraces development and worldwide impacts. Metropolitan focuses, like Auckland and Wellington, are centers of culinary innovativeness, where cooks draw motivation from nearby fixings and worldwide culinary patterns to make dishes that push the limits of taste.

In Auckland, a mixture of societies, voyagers can investigate restaurants that mix Kiwi fixings with Asian, Pacific, and European impacts. The outcome is a combination of flavors that mirrors the multicultural texture of New Zealand. From fish ceviche with local spices to sheep implanted with Center Eastern flavors, the cutting edge Kiwi combination scene welcomes guests to leave on a gastronomic experience that rises above conventional limits.

Specialty Lager Culture - A Brewmaster's Heaven:

New Zealand's specialty lager culture has encountered a renaissance, with a thriving number of breweries making one of a kind and delightful brews. From hoppy pale lagers to rich stouts, the specialty lager scene mirrors the Kiwi soul of development and an adoration for quality brews. Voyagers can drench themselves in this hoppy sanctuary, investigating distilleries that spot the open country and metropolitan scenes the same.

In the specialty lager capital of Wellington, known for its dynamic culinary scene, guests can set out on distillery visits that exhibit the craft of preparing. The fellowship among lager devotees, the tasting meetings, and the narratives shared by brewmasters make a vivid encounter that goes past the 16 ounces glass. Specialty brew turns into a social standard, exemplifying the Kiwi enthusiasm for greatness and a great time.

Difficulties and Manageability in Kiwi Food:

As New Zealand's culinary scene keeps on prospering, it likewise wrestles with the difficulties of maintainability, mindful obtaining, and the safeguarding of customary culinary information. The ubiquity of specific fixings, combined with the effects of environmental change, requires a smart way to deal with guarantee that Aotearoa's gastronomic legacy stays energetic for people in the future.

Endeavors to advance feasible fishing rehearses, support neighborhood ranchers, and lessen food squander are picking up speed. Gourmet experts and restaurateurs are progressively embracing the idea of "zero waste" kitchens, where each fixing is used to its fullest potential. The fragile harmony between fulfilling the hungers of local people and guests and shielding the country's normal assets is a story that keeps on unfurling inside New Zealand's culinary scene.

7.1 Explore New Zealand's unique culinary scene, featuring fresh and local ingredients.

A Culinary Odyssey through Aotearoa: Divulging the Kinds of New Zealand's Nearby Abundance

In the core of Aotearoa, New Zealand's culinary scene calls, offering a remarkable embroidery of flavors that reflect the different scenes of this island country. From the lavish fields of Waikato to the beach front overflow of Kaikoura, the culinary excursion through New Zealand is a festival of new, nearby fixings, where each dish portrays a story well established in the land. In this investigation, we disentangle the layers of New Zealand's culinary extravagance, a gastronomic odyssey that typifies the soul of "kai moana" (food from the ocean) and embraces the homestead to-table ethos with energy and imagination.

Ranch to-Table Customs:

New Zealand's culinary personality is profoundly laced with its obligation to cultivate to-table customs, where the excursion from farmsteads to kitchens is a story of supportability, newness, and a significant association with the land. In the peaceful scenes of Waikato, where verdant fields stretch as may be obvious, guests can submerge themselves in the core of dairy country.

The locale's dairy ranches, famous for delivering a-list cheeses, make their ways for voyagers anxious to investigate the specialty of cheesemaking. From rich blue cheeses to matured goudas, the tasting encounters are a demonstration of the nature of New Zealand's dairy items. The ranch to-table way of thinking stretches out past cheddar, incorporating a heap of privately obtained fixings that track down their direction onto the plates of both rustic bistros and metropolitan restaurants.

Practical Fish Blowouts:

As an island country embraced by the Pacific Sea, New Zealand's culinary embroidered artwork is woven with the wealth of its fish. The beach front town of Kaikoura, arranged on the South Island, remains as a demonstration of the wealth of kai moana. Here, guests can enjoy a fish feast that exhibits the sea's abundance in its most perfect structure.

Crawfish, paua (abalone), and blue cod become the overwhelming focus in Kaikoura's fish contributions.

Neighborhood restaurants, roosted along the shore, serve dishes that permit the kinds of the sea to sparkle. The obligation to supportable fishing rehearses guarantees that each nibble entices the taste buds as well as lines up with the ethos of dependable stewardship of marine assets.

Hangi Customs and Maori Culinary Legacy:

To get a handle on the quintessence of Kiwi cooking is to participate in the old Maori custom of hangi — a strategy for slow-preparing food in an earth broiler. The geothermal city of Rotorua, settled in the core of the North Island, gives a charming background to this culinary excursion into Maori legacy.

In Rotorua, the most common way of setting up a hangi is a scene that unfurls with accuracy. Privately obtained fixings, including meats, vegetables, and sweet treats, are put on warmed rocks covered in the earth, permitting them to cook gradually and assimilate the hearty flavors. The uncovering of the hangi isn't simply a culinary encounter; it is a festival of Maori friendliness and an association with the land that goes past the sense of taste.

Pavlova, the Quintessential Kiwi Treat:
No investigation of New Zealand's culinary scene is finished without enjoying pavlova — a famous treat that exemplifies the pleasantness of Kiwi customs. This meringue-based delicacy, enhanced with new leafy foods cream, mirrors the agreement among custom and advancement in New Zealand's culinary scene.

Pavlova's starting points might be bantered between New Zealand and Australia, yet its ubiquity in Kiwi families and bistros is undisputed. Whether delighted in the clamoring metropolitan bistros of Auckland or the curious ocean side restaurants of Dunedin, pavlova turns into a material for exhibiting the lively kinds of occasional foods grown from the ground imagination of Kiwi cooks.

High quality Wines: A Toast to Terroir:
New Zealand's obligation to greatness in winemaking has launch it onto the worldwide stage, with its Sauvignon Blancs, Pinot Noirs, and different varietals procuring global approval. The country's extraordinary terroir, portrayed by different microclimates and prolific soil, confers particular qualities to its wines, making each taste a tribute to Aotearoa's regular abundance.

In areas like Marlborough, where Sauvignon Blanc rules, guests can cross grape plantation loaded scenes and appreciate the products of fastidious viticulture. Tasting rooms offer a tactile excursion through the fresh whites and rich reds, giving experiences into the craftsmanship that changes grapes into fluid workmanship. Wine the travel industry turns into a road for interfacing with the land, the vintners, and the practices that make New Zealand's wines an essential piece of its culinary story.

Kumara, the Adaptable Yam:
Kumara, or yam, holds a loved spot in both Maori and Kiwi food. With its lively orange tissue and sweet, nutty flavor, kumara is a flexible fixing that highlights unmistakably in different dishes. From customary hangi to contemporary culinary manifestations, kumara is a demonstration of the variety and flexibility of New Zealand's gastronomy.

In the Hawke's Cove locale, where prolific soils and a warm environment make ideal circumstances for kumara development, guests can relish dishes that grandstand the yam's reach. Whether cooked, squashed, or integrated into creative treats, kumara mirrors the culinary inventiveness that characterizes Kiwi food.

Buzzy Honey bee Honey: Fluid Gold Experience:
New Zealand's flawless scenes add to its culinary lavishness as well as give a safe house to different widely varied vegetation. This biodiversity is reflected in the country's extraordinary honeys, with manuka honey standing apart as an image of Aotearoa's normal riches. The excursion from hive to jostle offers

an interesting look into the universe of beekeeping and the unpredictable cycle that changes nectar into fluid gold.

In the Cove of Bounty, guests can investigate honey homesteads where beekeepers tend to hives settled in the midst of local shrubbery. Directed visits demystify the specialty of beekeeping and permit visitors to taste a variety of honey assortments, each with its particular flavor profile. Manuka honey, commended for its indicated restorative properties, turns into a fluid gold sought after for its taste as well as for its potential medical advantages.

Present day Kiwi Combination: Culinary Development:

While customary flavors hold a unique spot, New Zealand's culinary scene likewise embraces development and worldwide impacts. Metropolitan focuses like Auckland and Wellington stand as centers of culinary inventiveness, where gourmet specialists draw motivation from neighborhood fixings and global culinary patterns to make dishes that push the limits of taste.

In Auckland, a city described by social variety, guests can investigate diners that mix Kiwi fixings with Asian, Pacific, and European impacts. The outcome is a combination of flavors that mirrors the multicultural texture of New Zealand. From fish ceviche with local spices to sheep imbued with Center Eastern flavors, the cutting edge Kiwi combination scene welcomes guests to set out on a gastronomic experience that rises above customary limits.

Specialty Lager Culture: A Brewmaster's Heaven:

New Zealand's specialty lager culture has encountered a renaissance, with a thriving number of bottling works creating one of a kind and delightful brews. From hoppy pale lagers to rich stouts, the specialty lager scene reflects the Kiwi soul of development and an adoration for quality blends. Voyagers can submerge themselves in this hoppy sanctuary, investigating bottling works that speck the open country and metropolitan scenes the same.

In the specialty lager capital of Wellington, known for its dynamic culinary scene, guests can set out on distillery visits that feature the craft of fermenting. The kinship among lager devotees, the tasting meetings, and the tales shared by brewmasters make a vivid encounter that goes past the 16 ounces glass. Specialty lager turns into a social standard, encapsulating the Kiwi energy for greatness and a great time.

Difficulties and Maintainability:

As New Zealand's culinary scene keeps on thriving, it wrestles with the difficulties of supportability, capable obtaining, and the protection of customary culinary information. The prominence of specific fixings, combined with the effects of environmental change, requires a smart way to deal with guarantee that Aotearoa's gastronomic legacy stays lively for people in the future.

Endeavors to advance manageable fishing rehearses, support nearby ranchers, and lessen food squander are picking up speed. Gourmet specialists and restaurateurs are progressively embracing the idea of "zero waste" kitchens, where each fixing is used to its fullest potential. The fragile harmony between fulfilling the cravings of local people and guests and shielding the country's regular assets is a story that keeps on unfurling inside New Zealand's culinary scene.

7.2 Highlight traditional Maori cuisine and the fusion of international influences.

Custom and Combination: The Culinary Embroidered artwork of Maori Cooking in Aotearoa

In the core of Aotearoa, the rich culinary embroidered artwork of New Zealand unfurls, woven with strings of custom and spiced up by the combination of worldwide impacts. Maori cooking, well established in the native culture of the Maori public, fills in as a tasty foundation in this gastronomic excursion. As we investigate the customary preferences that have endured for the long haul and the creative culinary mixes that reflect New Zealand's multicultural texture, we dig into the exceptional story of Maori food and its amicable concurrence with worldwide flavors.

Kai Maori: The Substance of Conventional Maori Foodways:

Kai Maori, or Maori food, is an impression of the profound association the Maori public have with their tribal terrains and waters. The culinary customs have been gone down through ages, protecting the flavors and strategies that characterize the quintessence of Maori food. One of the most notorious and customary cooking techniques is the hangi, an earth stove planning that includes slow-preparing food over warmed rocks covered in the ground.

The hangi isn't just a strategy for cooking; a social custom unites networks. Meats, vegetables, and now and again fish are painstakingly layered in crates, covered with leaves, and left to implant with the hearty smell of the earth broiler.

The uncovering of the hangi is a festival, a second where the kinds of the land and the work of collective planning meet into a banquet that rises above the domain of food.

The Abundance of the Ocean: Fish in Maori Food:

Maori food draws vigorously from the bountiful fish that encompasses the islands of New Zealand. Kai moana, signifying "food from the ocean," is a demonstration of the respect Maori individuals have for the sea's contributions. Customary dishes include staples like paua (abalone), kina (ocean imp), and different types of fish.

Paua, a valued delicacy with an unmistakable flavor and surface, frequently tracks down its direction into wastes or is delighted in essentially, permitting the normal taste of the ocean to sparkle. Kina, with its briny extravagance, might be integrated into stews or utilized as a fixing for exquisite dishes. The incorporation of these fish delights reflects not just the Maori nation's dependence on the sea for food yet in addition their profound regard for the fragile equilibrium of marine environments.

Kumara and Root Vegetables: The Land's Abundance:

The Maori relationship with the land is similarly appeared in the utilization of native vegetables, with kumara (yam) being a foundation of Maori food. Kumara, with its energetic orange shade and sweet, nutty flavor, is a flexible fixing that highlights conspicuously in both customary and contemporary Maori dishes.

Whether broiled, crushed, or integrated into stews, kumara fills in as an image of food and social importance. The development of kumara requires a profound comprehension of the land's cycles, mirroring the interconnectedness between the Maori public and the earth they occupy. The root vegetables, like taro and sweet potatoes, further add to the wealth of Maori culinary customs, giving a different exhibit of flavors and surfaces.

Acquaintance of the Hangi with Worldwide Crowds:

While conventional Maori food has been saved inside the networks, the idea of the hangi has likewise tracked down its direction onto the global stage, charming crowds with its novel cooking technique and social importance. Far-reaching developments, celebrations, and, surprisingly, fancy foundations have embraced the hangi, acquainting a more extensive crowd with the kinds of customary Maori cooking.

In metropolitan places like Auckland and Wellington, gourmet specialists have creatively adjusted the hangi procedure to make contemporary dishes that honor Maori customs while imbuing a cutting edge culinary energy. This combination of customary strategies with contemporary show features the versatility and dynamism of Maori cooking, welcoming the two local people and guests to encounter the profundity of flavors established in social legacy.

Worldwide Impacts and the Blend of Kiwi Food:

The culinary scene of New Zealand is a demonstration of the nation's multiculturalism, and Maori cooking assumes a crucial part in forming the by and large gastronomic personality. The combination of worldwide impacts, from European to Asian to Pacific Edge flavors, has made a blend that improves the Kiwi culinary experience.

In metropolitan center points like Auckland, where various networks coincide, the combination of Maori fixings with worldwide procedures has led to a contemporary Maori food. Culinary experts, motivated by the regular abundance of New Zealand and the worldwide storage space, explore different avenues regarding customary fixings in creative ways. The outcome is a culinary excursion that overcomes any barrier among legacy and innovation, permitting customary Maori flavors to sparkle close by worldwide culinary patterns.

Hangi-Roused Combination: Reevaluating Custom:

The hangi, with its profound social roots, has turned into a wellspring of motivation for gourmet experts looking to rethink custom in contemporary settings. Cafés across New Zealand, especially in vacationer locations, offer hangi-propelled dishes that catch the quintessence of the earth broiler cooking technique while introducing it in a refined and open way.

Current translations of the hangi may include slow-cooked meats mixed with customary spices and flavors, gave a contemporary plating tasteful. The masterfulness lies in respecting the social meaning of the hangi while adjusting it to suit the developing sense of taste of the two local people and worldwide guests. This combination not just acquaints customary Maori flavors with a more extensive crowd yet additionally cultivates an appreciation for the rich embroidery of New Zealand's culinary legacy.

Social Celebrations and Culinary Festivals:

Social celebrations and culinary festivals assume a crucial part in exhibiting the variety of Maori cooking. Occasions like the Wild Food Celebration and the Hokitika Wildfoods Celebration give a stage to gourmet experts and food lovers to investigate creative approaches to integrating conventional Maori fixings into contemporary dishes.

These celebrations become a powerful space where the combination of worldwide and Maori flavors is praised, offering participants an opportunity to encounter the developing scene of New Zealand's culinary scene. Whether it's hangi-implanted road food or kai moana-roused tapas, these occasions add to the continuous story of Maori cooking, guaranteeing its significance in a cutting edge, worldwide setting.

Worldwide Acknowledgment and Native Culinary Pride:

Lately, there has been a developing worldwide acknowledgment of native foods, including Maori cooking, as culinary fortunes that add to the world's gastronomic variety. The focus on customary fixings, cooking techniques, and narrating has raised Maori food to a place of pride, inside New Zealand as well as on the worldwide culinary stage.

Worldwide food lovers and culinary travelers search out credible Maori feasting encounters, spurring an interest for cafés and restaurants that focus on customary fixings and readiness procedures. The worldwide appreciation for Maori cooking stretches out past the plate, encouraging a feeling of social pride and character for the Maori public.

Maintainability and Conventional Insight:

The standards of manageability implanted in customary Maori rehearses line up with contemporary endeavors to advance eco-cognizant eating. The Maori nation's all encompassing way to deal with food, which includes a profound comprehension of the interconnectedness between land, ocean, and food, reverberates with the cutting edge talk on economical and moral eating.

The resurgence of interest in native fixings and conventional insight in regards to gathering and rummaging lines up with the more extensive worldwide development toward cognizant utilization. Maori cooking becomes a culinary excursion as well as an example in manageability, helping us to remember the significance of regarding the climate and safeguarding conventional information for people in the future.

7.3 Discuss the role of food in connecting with the culture and history of the region.

Culinary Narratives: Investigating the Social and Authentic Embroidered artwork Through Food

In the core of any district lies a culinary scene that fills in as a passage to its way of life and history. New Zealand, with its different social impacts and rich history, offers a gastronomic excursion that rises above simple food. Food, in the entirety of its structures, assumes a significant part in associating people with the stories of the past, the customs of the present, and the developing personality of the district. As we leave on a tangible investigation, we dig into the complex connection among food and the social and verifiable embroidery of Aotearoa.

Native Roots: Maori Food as Social Legacy:

To see New Zealand's social and verifiable story through food, one should start with the native Maori individuals and their culinary customs. Maori food, well established in the harmonious connection between the land and its kin, turns into a vessel for saving and communicating social legacy across ages.

Conventional Maori dishes, for example, those arranged through the hangi cooking technique, reverberation hundreds of years of practices profoundly entwined with the land. The hangi, with its sluggish cooking strategy utilizing warmed rocks covered in the earth, isn't just a culinary cycle however a social custom that typifies the substance of Maori friendliness. Through the kinds of hangi-cooked meats, root vegetables like kumara, and fish treats, people participate in a tactile excursion that associates them with the Maori perspective, where the earth, ocean, and food are joined.

Social Celebrations and Culinary Festivals: Living History on a Plate:

Social celebrations and culinary festivals become living accounts that unfurl the area's set of experiences and various social impacts. Occasions like the Wild Food Celebration and the Hokitika Wildfoods Celebration grandstand not just the development of New Zealand's culinary scene yet additionally the combination of conventional Maori flavors with worldwide impacts.

In these energetic festivals, participants experience the reverberation of authentic stories through dishes that span the past and the present. Whether it's the recovery of antiquated Maori fixings or the combination of pioneer impacts, these culinary social affairs become stages for social trade and narrating, welcoming people to taste the set of experiences on their plates.

Pilgrim Inheritance: European Effects on Kiwi Food:

The pilgrim time, set apart by European settlement in New Zealand, made a permanent imprint on the district's culinary scene. European impacts, especially English, presented new fixings, cooking methods, and flavor profiles that became incorporated into Kiwi food.

The notable evening tea, with its sensitive cakes and scones, mirrors a custom acquired from pilgrim times. The idea of dishes, pies, and stews reflects the generous passage brought by European pilgrims. The persevering through prominence of dishes like fried fish and French fries, shepherd's pie, and the quintessential New Zealand meat pie gives proper respect to this pioneer inheritance, making a culinary extension to a common history that keeps on molding New Zealand's food culture.

Pacific Combination: Impacts from the Islands:

Past European impacts, New Zealand's area in the South Pacific positions it to embrace the kinds of the more extensive Pacific locale. Polynesian and Melanesian culinary impacts, exuding from the islands of the Pacific, add to the dynamic embroidery of Kiwi cooking.

Fixings like coconut, taro, and tropical organic products track down their direction into contemporary dishes, making a Pacific combination that gives proper respect to the interconnectedness of the Pacific people groups. Pacific Islander people group, with their interesting culinary practices, add layers of intricacy and variety to New Zealand's food scene, helping people to remember the nation's connections to the more extensive Pacific family.

Settler Stories: Worldwide Effects on Kiwi Plates:

New Zealand's set of experiences is set apart by influxes of migration that have carried assorted social impacts to its shores. Every settler bunch, whether from Asia, the Center East, or somewhere else, has contributed not exclusively to the social texture of New Zealand yet additionally to its culinary scene.

In metropolitan habitats like Auckland, known for its social variety, people can set out on a worldwide culinary excursion without leaving as far as possible. Asian night markets, Center Eastern diners, and the fragrant flavors of Indian cooking act as tokens of the multiculturalism that characterizes present day New Zealand. Through the kinds of foreigner foods, people associate with the tales of versatility, variation, and the continuous advancement of Kiwi character.

Ranch to-Table: Appreciating the Abundance of the Land:

New Zealand's rural lavishness and obligation to manageable practices are essential to its homestead to-table development. The idea of obtaining fixings locally, frequently from limited scope makers, advances ecological maintainability as well as permits people to draw in with the accounts of the land.

In districts like Waikato, where lavish fields flourish, ranch visits and visits to high quality cheddar makers give looks into the horticultural legacy of the area. Ranchers' business sectors become dynamic center points where people associate with cultivators, makers, and the occasional rhythms of the land. By relishing the results of New Zealand's fruitful soils, people participate in a tactile investigation that goes past taste, connecting them to the rural stories that have molded the locale for quite a long time.

Culinary The travel industry: An Excursion Through Time and Flavor:

The ascent of culinary the travel industry in New Zealand mirrors a developing longing among voyagers to interface with the social and verifiable stories of an objective through its food. From directed wine visits in the grape plantation loaded scenes of Marlborough to vivid encounters in Maori hangi readiness, culinary the travel industry turns into a course for people to investigate the district's complex history and social variety.

In areas like Hawke's Cove, eminent for its winemaking, guests could not just relish at any point grant winning wines yet in addition enjoy connoisseur encounters that grandstand the locale's culinary ability. Through active cooking classes, visits to high quality makers, and directed tastings, culinary sightseers become dynamic members in New Zealand's gastronomic story, improving their movement experience with the kinds of the land.

Safeguarding Customs: Culinary Legacy as Social Inheritance:

As New Zealand explores the flows of globalization and modernization, the protection of culinary customs becomes principal in defending social heritages.

Drives to record, celebrate, and communicate customary recipes, cooking procedures, and food ceremonies guarantee that people in the future can keep on associating with the set of experiences and culture of the locale through food.

In provincial networks, endeavors to restore antiquated Maori fixings, like the utilization of local spices and greeneries, add to the safeguarding of native culinary information. In like manner, the documentation of frontier recipes and foreigner dishes turns into a method for regarding the different strings that have woven together to make the embroidery of Kiwi cooking.

Feasible Practices: Gastronomy as Ecological Stewardship:

The contemporary talk on supportability and ecological stewardship converges flawlessly with the culinary scene of New Zealand. The consciousness of the effect of food decisions on the climate has prompted a reliable way to deal with eating that lines up with verifiable acts of cleverness and regard for nature.

Cafés and restaurants embracing economical practices, from limiting food waste to focusing on neighborhood and occasional fixings, epitomize a pledge to dependable eating. By picking such foundations, people enjoy the kinds of the district as well as conform to a more extensive story of natural cognizance and verifiable regard for the land.

CHAPTER 8

"Conservation Chronicles"

Preservation Narratives: Supporting Nature's Heritage in New Zealand
In the core of Aotearoa, New Zealand, an enamoring story unfurls — a story of responsibility, stewardship, and a steady devotion to safeguarding the flawless magnificence of the land. This is the Protection Narratives, a story that rises above existence, winding around together accounts of preservation endeavors that have turned into an essential piece of New Zealand's character. In a nation where the scenes are however various as they seem to be stunning, the protection venture is a continuous adventure that mirrors the aggregate responsibility of Kiwis to shield their normal legacy.

The Ensemble of Scenes: Aotearoa's Normal Brilliant qualities:
New Zealand's scenes read like an ensemble of nature's works of art, each note formed by the components and the progression of time. From the transcending pinnacles of the Southern Alps to the fjords of Fiordland, and from the geothermal miracles of Rotorua to the brilliant sea shores of the Coromandel Promontory, Aotearoa is a material painted with different biological systems and special biodiversity.

The Preservation Narratives start with a profound appreciation for this regular quality — an acknowledgment that these scenes are a wellspring of beautiful miracle as well as environments for a huge number of vegetation found no place else on The planet. From old kahikatea backwoods to the lively birdlife, including the notable kiwi, the preservation venture is a pledge to guarantee that these fortunes persevere for a long time into the future.

The Kiwi's Call: Notorious Species and Image of Preservation:
At the core of New Zealand's preservation endeavors stands a padded symbol — the kiwi. This flightless, nighttime bird, with its particular outline and tormenting call, typifies the one of a kind avian fauna that graces the islands. In any case, the kiwi, alongside numerous other local species, faces the danger of elimination because of presented hunters and living space misfortune.

Preservation drives, both government-drove and local area driven, center around safeguarding the kiwi and its environment. From hunter free islands to broad catching projects on the central area, New Zealanders have revitalized together to make asylums where these notable birds can flourish. The kiwi's endurance isn't simply a preservation objective; it is an image of New Zealanders' obligation to safeguarding their regular legacy.

Island Safe-havens: A Shelter for Local Animal groups:

Island asylums arise as encouraging signs in the Preservation Accounts, offering places of refuge where local vegetation can prosper without the danger of presented hunters. Ulva Island, Kapiti Island, and the hunter free safe house of Tiritiri Matangi are only a couple of instances of islands that have been fastidiously reestablished and secured.

These safe-havens are residing research centers of preservation, where imperiled species track down asylum, and environments are permitted to recover. The arrival of birdlife, the thriving of local plants, and the fragile dance of nature's equilibrium unfurl as examples of overcoming adversity in these safe-havens. The Preservation Accounts commend these island shelters as microcosms of what is conceivable when human assurance meets the versatility of nature.

Hunter Free New Zealand: An Intense Vision Unfurling:

The vision of a hunter free New Zealand, while aggressive, is at the front of the Preservation Narratives. The presentation of mammalian hunters, like stoats, rodents, and possums, has unleashed destruction on the country's local biodiversity. Hunter Free 2050, a public drive, means to free New Zealand of these obtrusive dangers, permitting local species to flourish.

Local area drove catching projects, inventive vermin control innovations, and the joint effort between government offices and ecological associations are driving the hunter free plan. The Preservation Narratives catch the aggregate work to transform this venturesome vision into a reality, perceiving that the end of hunters isn't simply a biological objective yet a demonstration of the Kiwi soul of versatility and assurance.

Te Araroa: A Path of Protection and Association:

As the Protection Annals unfurl, the story interlaces with Te Araroa — the Long Pathway that traverses the length of New Zealand. This ceaseless path, extending from Cape Reinga in the North to Feign in the South, fills in as a figurative and actual excursion through the different scenes of Aotearoa.

Te Araroa isn't simply a path for explorers; it is a pathway for protection and association. Explorers navigate through public parks, seaside strolls, and local woodlands, seeing the excellence of immaculate scenes and the continuous protection endeavors en route. The path turns into a living demonstration of the fragile harmony between human diversion and the conservation of normal environments, welcoming people to be the two observers and stewards of the land.

Kauri Dieback: The Fight to Save Antiquated Goliaths:

The Protection Narratives likewise wrestle with a cutting edge danger that reverberations through old woodlands — the kauri dieback infection. Kauri trees, transcending goliaths that have represented hundreds of years, face a staggering microbe that undermines their actual presence. The fight against kauri dieback turns into a piercing section in the protection adventure, as researchers, moderates, and the public meet up to track down arrangements.

Track terminations, cleanliness stations, and examination into sickness safe kauri become piece of the arms stockpile in the battle against this minuscule enemy. The Preservation Annals perceive the direness of tending to prompt dangers as well as arising difficulties that endanger the strength of New Zealand's normal legacy.

Environmental Change and Protection Difficulties: A Call to Transformation:

In the developing parts of the Preservation Annals, the phantom of environmental change poses a potential threat. Aotearoa, similar to the remainder of the world, wrestles with the effects of a changing environment — from modified weather conditions to rising ocean levels. Preservation endeavors should adjust to these new difficulties, perceiving that the security of biodiversity is complicatedly connected to the wellbeing and strength of environments.

Environment tough preservation procedures, supportable land the board practices, and local area commitment in environment variation become essential parts of the Protection Narratives. The interconnectedness of natural frameworks and the more extensive worldwide setting push New Zealanders into a proactive position, tending to the diverse difficulties presented by an evolving environment.

Social Preservation: Maori Guardianship of the Land:

In the Protection Narratives, the Maori idea of kaitiakitanga arises as a core value — a way of thinking of guardianship and obligation regarding the normal world. Maori culture, profoundly interlaced with the land and its assets, stresses an all encompassing way to deal with preservation that perceives the interconnectedness of every single living thing.

Conventional information, went down through ages, illuminates contemporary protection rehearses. The combination of Maori viewpoints in preservation navigation becomes an issue of strategy as well as an impression of a social ethos that sees the land as a taonga (treasure) to be safeguarded for people in the future. The Protection Narratives commend the beneficial interaction between social preservation and biological stewardship, perceiving the significance of integrating native insight into current protection procedures.

Instructive Drives: Sustaining the Preservation Ethos:

Training turns into a foundation in the Preservation Narratives, as supporting a protection ethos in people in the future becomes fundamental. From school programs that draw in understudies in involved protection ventures to intuitive guest communities that give environmental information, training turns into a vehicle for imparting a feeling of obligation and association with the land.

Resident science drives, where people in general effectively partakes in observing and protection endeavors, highlight the conviction that preservation isn't the sole liability of government organizations yet an aggregate undertaking. The Preservation Narratives feature the force of information and mindfulness in encouraging a general public that qualities and safeguards its regular legacy.

Marine Preservation: Gatekeepers of the Sea Domain:

As the Preservation Annals navigate from land to the ocean, the significance of marine protection becomes the overwhelming focus. New Zealand, encompassed by immense seas, flaunts assorted marine environments, from the rich waters of the Hauraki Bay to the subantarctic areas abounding with marine life. Marine stores, practical fisheries the executives, and endeavors to battle marine contamination become necessary components in the preservation account.

The guardianship of the seas stretches out past regional waters, with New Zealand assuming a part in worldwide marine preservation arrangements. The Preservation Annals unfurl underneath the waves, perceiving that the soundness of the sea is indivisible from the prosperity of the whole planet.

The travel industry and Preservation: Finding Some kind of harmony:

The travel industry, while an essential piece of New Zealand's economy, presents the two valuable open doors and difficulties in the Preservation Narratives. The appeal of Aotearoa's scenes draws a great many guests every year, giving a financial motivator to preservation endeavors. Be that as it may, the deluge of vacationers likewise puts tension on delicate biological systems and requires a sensitive harmony among conservation and openness.

The Preservation Accounts investigate maintainable the travel industry drives, dependable travel rehearses, and the job of the travel industry administrators as stewards of the land. The objective is to guarantee that the advantages of the travel industry add to preservation instead of give and take the very loves that draw in guests.

The Incomplete Ensemble of Protection:

The Preservation Annals, a story carved in the scenes and seascapes of Aotearoa, stay an incomplete orchestra — a demonstration of the continuous responsibility of New Zealanders to protect their regular heritage. From the mountain edges to the sea profundities, from local area drove undertakings to public drives, the parts of protection unfurl as time passes.

The story perceives that difficulties continue, new dangers arise, and the amicable harmony among people and nature requires steady transformation. The Preservation Narratives are stories of wins as well as affirmations of the intricacies intrinsic in the stewardship of a biodiverse country. In the possession of the caretakers of Aotearoa, the incomplete orchestra of protection resounds with trust, strength, and an assurance to guarantee that the scenes, environments, and species that characterize New Zealand persevere for a long time into the future.

8.1 Discuss New Zealand's commitment to environmental conservation.

Gatekeepers of Aotearoa: New Zealand's Unfaltering Obligation to Natural Preservation

In the core of the South Pacific, settled between the Tasman Ocean and the Pacific Sea, lies a country that has turned into a worldwide reference point for ecological protection — New Zealand, or Aotearoa in the Maori language. This island country, famous for its stunning scenes and remarkable biodiversity, has carved its obligation to protection profound into its social and political texture. The tale of New Zealand's devotion to ecological protection isn't just one of strategy and practice; a story mirrors the aggregate ethos of a country that considers itself to be the watchman of its regular fortunes.

A Social Embroidery Woven with Protection Strings:

To see New Zealand's obligation to ecological protection, one must initially unwind the strings of its social woven artwork. The Maori public, the native occupants of Aotearoa, have long held a significant association with the land and ocean.

The idea of kaitiakitanga, or guardianship, is implanted in Maori culture — a way of thinking that stresses the obligation of people to really focus on and safeguard the climate.

This social ethos has pervaded contemporary New Zealand society, impacting everything from government arrangements to grassroots preservation drives. The obligation to natural stewardship isn't just a question of regulation; it is a statement of a firmly established conviction that the prosperity of the land is entwined with the prosperity of individuals.

Spearheading Protection Developments: Setting the Stage:

New Zealand's obligation to natural preservation has profound authentic roots, set apart by spearheading developments that set up for current protection rehearses. The late nineteenth and mid twentieth hundreds of years saw the foundation of stores and public parks, driven by an acknowledgment of the need to save the country's interesting vegetation.

The formation of Tongariro Public Park in 1887, the main public park in New Zealand and the Southern Side of the equator, denoted an achievement in the worldwide preservation development. This early obligation to safeguarding normal scenes established the groundwork for the protection ethos that would develop throughout the long term.

Milestone Regulation: A Structure for Protection:

The twentieth century saw the rise of milestone regulation that cemented New Zealand's obligation to preservation. The foundation of the Division of Protection (DOC) in 1987 was a critical second — a committed organization entrusted with overseeing and rationing the nation's normal and memorable legacy.

Regulation, for example, the Preservation Act 1987 and the Public Parks Act 1980 gave the lawful structure to protection the board. These demonstrations framed the standards of preservation, stressing the assurance of normal and memorable assets, the support of biodiversity, and the arrangement of chances for diversion and pleasure in these fortunes.

Hunter Free New Zealand 2050: A Daring Vision:

One of the most daring articulations of New Zealand's obligation to natural preservation is the Hunter Free New Zealand 2050 drive. Sent off in 2016, this aggressive undertaking means to free the nation of presented hunters like rodents, stoats, and possums continuously 2050. These obtrusive species represent a critical danger to local birdlife, bugs, and vegetation, adding to the decay of native biological systems.

The Hunter Free 2050 vision mirrors an intense assurance to reestablish the regular equilibrium and safeguard jeopardized species. Local area drove catching projects, propels in bug control advancements, and examination into hereditary arrangements are all essential for the multi-layered technique. This bold vision isn't simply a preservation drive; it is a public obligation to recovering Aotearoa's status as a safe-haven for interesting biodiversity.

Local area Drove Preservation: Grassroots Guardianship:

The obligation to natural preservation in New Zealand stretches out past government organizations to the very networks that possess the scenes. Local area drove protection projects have turned into a main thrust in shielding nearby biological systems. From bug control drives in rural regions to the rebuilding of wetlands and local plantings, networks the nation over effectively take part in the guardianship of their surroundings.

The development of Protection Sheets, comprised of nearby workers, embodies this grassroots commitment. These sheets work in organization with the DOC, giving important nearby information and adding to preservation navigation. The outcome of local area drove drives highlights that protection isn't the sole liability of legislative bodies however an aggregate undertaking that requires the dynamic inclusion of people and networks.

Marine Preservation: Safeguarding Maritime Wealth:

New Zealand's obligation to preservation stretches out past earthly scenes to the immense blue breadths encompass its islands. Marine preservation assumes a significant part in safeguarding the country's different marine environments. Marine stores, where fishing and other extractive exercises are limited, act as shelters for marine life to flourish.

The Hauraki Bay Marine Park, laid out in 2000, represents New Zealand's devotion to saving its maritime wealth. This marine park, enveloping the waters around Auckland, perceives the interconnectedness of land and ocean. Endeavors to battle marine contamination, direct business fishing, and safeguard jeopardized marine species further highlight the country's obligation to all encompassing protection that traverses both earthbound and marine conditions.

Environmental Change Relief and Transformation: A Proactive Position:
Notwithstanding worldwide environmental change, New Zealand has taken on a proactive position, perceiving the significance of moderating ozone depleting substance discharges and adjusting to changing climatic circumstances. The New Zealand Government has focused on progressing to a low-outflow, environment strong economy. Arrangements and drives expect to diminish outflows from farming, change to sustainable power sources, and upgrade the strength of networks to environment related influences.

The protection ethos crosses with environment activity, as solid biological systems add to carbon sequestration, biodiversity flexibility, and the general transformation limit of the climate. The obligation to environmental change moderation and variation mirrors a comprehensive comprehension of preservation that goes past the security of individual species or scenes.

Saving Biodiversity: A Worldwide Obligation:
New Zealand's obligation to ecological protection isn't kept to its lines; it reaches out to a worldwide obligation regarding saving biodiversity.

The country effectively participates in global preservation endeavors, perceiving that large numbers of its local species are transient and that biological systems are interconnected across landmasses.

Support in worldwide arrangements and drives, like the Show on Natural Variety, exhibits New Zealand's obligation to cooperative preservation. The nation use its mastery in island reclamation, bother control, and native preservation practices to add to worldwide biodiversity protection.

Supportable Agribusiness and Land Use: Adjusting Creation and Protection:
New Zealand's economy has for some time been interlaced with horticulture, and the obligation to protection stretches out to finding a harmony between useful land use and ecological conservation. Reasonable horticulture works on, including drives to diminish supplement spillover, safeguard streams, and advance regenerative cultivating, mirror a pledge to guaranteeing that the land stays useful without compromising environmental respectability.

The acknowledgment that protection and horticulture are not fundamentally unrelated yet can be blended is a demonstration of the country's devotion to tracking down inventive answers for complex difficulties. This approach lines up with the comprehension that the prosperity of provincial networks is unpredictably connected to the wellbeing of the land they develop.

Instructive Drives: Supporting Preservation Values:

A fundamental part of New Zealand's obligation to ecological preservation lies in instructive drives that sustain protection values in the more youthful age. From school programs that integrate ecological training into the educational plan to drives that give outside opportunities for growth, instruction turns into a foundation for imparting a feeling of obligation and association with the land.

Zoos, natural life safe-havens, and intelligent guest habitats likewise assume a part in encouraging ecological mindfulness. These spaces grandstand New Zealand's novel biodiversity as well as teach guests about the significance of protection and the moves they can make to add to shielding the climate.

Difficulties and Valuable open doors: Exploring the Preservation Scene:

While New Zealand's obligation to ecological preservation is excellent, it doesn't come without difficulties. Obtrusive species, environment misfortune, and the continuous effect of human exercises present determined dangers to the country's biological systems. Environmental change presents new intricacies, requiring versatile systems to relieve its belongings.

Notwithstanding, inside these difficulties lie open doors for advancement, cooperation, and ceaseless improvement. The Preservation Annals of New Zealand are dynamic, steadily developing stories that mirror the strength of a country despite natural vulnerabilities.

The obligation to preservation is definitely not a static statement however a no nonsense ethos that answers arising difficulties sincerely and versatility.

An Orchestra of Guardianship:

In the orchestra of natural preservation, New Zealand remains as a director, directing the country toward an amicable relationship with the land and ocean. The obligation to preservation is definitely not a solitary demonstration however an ensemble of different drives, viewpoints, and values that unite to make an aggregate ethos of guardianship.

From the snow-covered pinnacles of the Southern Alps to the unblemished waters of Fiordland, and from the old kahikatea woodlands to the brilliant sea shores of the Coromandel, New Zealand's scenes are not simply picturesque vistas — they are demonstrations of the continuous obligation to safeguard the country's regular legacy.

As the Protection Narratives unfurl, they uncover an account of kaitiakitanga — a social way of thinking of guardianship that rises above ages. New Zealand's obligation to natural preservation is a promise to be stewards of the land, defenders of biodiversity, and caretakers of an inheritance that traverses centuries. In the possession of Kiwis, youthful and old, the orchestra of guardianship keeps on playing, resounding across mountains and seas, repeating a promise to protecting Aotearoa's regular fortunes for the ages on the way.

8.2 Explore initiatives to protect native species and restore ecosystems.

Shielding Fortunes: Drives to Safeguard Local Species and Reestablish Environments in New Zealand

In the complex embroidery of New Zealand's scenes, a significant obligation to safeguarding local species and reestablishing biological systems winds through the texture of the country. Aotearoa, with its one of a kind biodiversity and native vegetation, has turned into a worldwide model in protection endeavors. This investigation digs into the drives attempted to shield local species and revive environments, exhibiting the multi-layered approach that characterizes New Zealand's preservation scene.

Hunter Free New Zealand: A Spearheading Vision:

At the front of New Zealand's drives to safeguard local species is the nervy vision of a Hunter Free New Zealand by 2050. Presented hunters, like rodents, stoats, and possums, have presented extreme dangers to the country's endemic birdlife and biological systems. The Hunter Free 2050 drive is a fantastic obligation to dispose of these obtrusive species completely, permitting local vegetation to flourish.

Local area drove catching projects, propels in bug control advances, and creative hereditary arrangements are necessary parts of the Hunter Free 2050 methodology. The drive exemplifies New Zealand's purpose to recover its status as a safe-haven for exceptional biodiversity and fills in as an energizing point for networks, specialists, and policymakers in the common mission of killing presented hunters.

Island Asylums: Shelters for Jeopardized Species:

Islands, both huge and little, have become asylums where New Zealand's local species find shelter from the dangers presented by presented hunters. Ulva Island, off the bank of Stewart Island, remains as a demonstration of the progress of such island safe-havens. When tormented by intrusive species, Ulva Island went through thorough vermin destruction endeavors, changing it into a shelter for jeopardized birds, reptiles, and plants.

Kapiti Island, situated off the Kapiti Coast, is one more model of island protection. This hunter free safe-haven gives a protected living space to species like the little spotted kiwi, takahe, and kaka. The outcome of these island safe-havens highlights the viability of confining biological systems from obtrusive dangers, permitting local species to recuperate and flourish in a safeguarded climate.

Central area Islands: Fencing Out Dangers:

Broadening the idea of island safe-havens to the central area, New Zealand has spearheaded the improvement of central area islands — enormous regions encased by resistant to hunter walls. These walls go about as hindrances, keeping presented hunters from getting to and hurting local species inside the encased regions.

Zealandia, a 225-hectare metropolitan ecosanctuary in Wellington, is a great representation of a central area island. Encircled by a hunter resistant wall, Zealandia has given a place of refuge to local birds, reptiles, and plants. The progress of this drive has prodded the foundation of comparable central area islands, exhibiting an imaginative way to deal with making safeguarded spaces inside bigger scenes.

Preservation Canines: Releasing Canine Ability for Insurance:

In the unpredictable dance of preservation, canines have arisen as surprising partners in the endeavors to safeguard local species. Preservation canines, profoundly prepared canines with an intense feeling of smell, assume an essential part in identifying and making progressives aware of the presence of obtrusive species. These extraordinarily prepared canines are sent in different protection programs, from distinguishing kiwi homes to finding the presence of hunters.

The utilization of protection canines isn't just an effective and painless strategy for checking natural life yet in addition a demonstration of the flexibility of preservation systems. These four-legged watchmen embody the imagination and cleverness implanted in New Zealand's obligation to safeguarding its one of a kind environments.

Reclamation of Wetlands: Supporting Biodiversity Areas of interest:

Wetlands, vital biodiversity areas of interest, have been the focal point of broad rebuilding endeavors in New Zealand. By and large, numerous wetlands were depleted for rural purposes, prompting the deficiency of important natural surroundings for local species. Reclamation drives try to switch this pattern by reestablishing regular water stream, establishing local vegetation, and controlling intrusive species.

The Whangamarino Wetland, one of New Zealand's biggest leftover marsh wetlands, is a perfect representation of fruitful rebuilding. Endeavors to replant local species, control bug species, and team up with nearby networks have added to the recuperation of this fundamental wetland biological system. The rebuilding of wetlands sustains biodiversity as well as upgrades water quality and gives significant environment administrations.

Kauri Dieback The executives: Safeguarding Old Goliaths:

The fight against kauri dieback sickness addresses a particular protection challenge in New Zealand. Kauri trees, old goliaths that have represented hundreds of years, face a minuscule microorganism that undermines their endurance. Endeavors to oversee and relieve the spread of kauri dieback include a blend of track terminations, cleanliness stations, and examination into sickness safe kauri.

The Waipoua Woods, home to probably the biggest kauri trees, has turned into a point of convergence for kauri dieback the board. Here, the sensitive harmony between permitting free to see the value in these old monsters and shielding the trees from the gamble of illness transmission is a demonstration of the nuanced idea of preservation choices.

Biodiversity Passageways: Associating Living spaces for Flexibility:

Perceiving the significance of keeping up with associated territories for strong environments, New Zealand has embraced the idea of biodiversity hallways. These halls, frequently comprising of local plantings, intend to connect divided environments, permitting local species to move openly between regions. The rebuilding of hallways upgrades hereditary variety, works with normal movement, and gives untamed life safe pathways across scenes.

The Hunua Reaches in Auckland highlight a biodiversity passage drive, where local plantings along streams and revegetation projects interface divided environments. By encouraging network, these halls add to the drawn out suitability of local species and advance biological system flexibility despite ecological difficulties.

Riparian Planting: Sustaining Streamside Environments:

Riparian zones, the regions along conduits, assume a urgent part in supporting freshwater environments. Riparian establishing drives center around reestablishing local vegetation along streams and streams, forestalling disintegration, further developing water quality, and giving natural surroundings to amphibian and earthbound species.

The Whangawehi Catchment The board Gathering on the North Island represents the outcome of riparian establishing projects. Cooperative endeavors between nearby networks, ranchers, and preservation associations have prompted the rebuilding of streamside natural surroundings, helping both earthbound and sea-going biodiversity. These drives mirror a comprehensive way to deal with protection that perceives the interconnectedness of land and water environments.

Local area Preservation Undertakings: Engaging Stewards of the Land:

New Zealand's obligation to safeguarding local species reaches out past legislative and institutional endeavors to the very networks that occupy the scenes. Local area preservation projects engage nearby occupants to become stewards of their surroundings, cultivating a feeling of pride and obligation regarding the prosperity of local widely varied vegetation.

Project Dark red, a local area drove drive zeroed in on the rebuilding of local pohutukawa and rata trees, embodies the force of grassroots protection. By drawing in networks in planting and really focusing on local trees, Venture

Dark red adds to biological system rebuilding as well as imparts a feeling of satisfaction and association with New Zealand's regular legacy.

Hostage Rearing Projects: Protecting Jeopardized Species:

For species near the very edge of termination, hostage reproducing programs have turned into a life saver. New Zealand has executed such projects to save and safeguard imperiled species, giving an impermanent sanctuary to them while tending to the dangers they face in nature.

The kākāpō, a fundamentally jeopardized parrot, is a point of convergence of hostage reproducing endeavors. With just a modest bunch of people staying in the wild, concentrated preservation measures, including living space security and hunter control, are supplemented by a painstakingly overseen hostage rearing project. These projects intend to reinforce populace numbers and once again introduce species to their regular natural surroundings whenever dangers have been relieved.

Mātauranga Māori in Protection: Native Insight in real life:

Inserted inside New Zealand's preservation drives is the mix of Mātauranga Māori — the conventional information and astuteness of the Maori public. Māori viewpoints on protection underline the interconnectedness of every single living thing and the all encompassing way to deal with ecological stewardship.

The Whio Everlastingly program, zeroed in on the protection of the whio (blue duck), embodies the joining of Mātauranga Māori. Cooperation with neighborhood iwi (clans), fuse of customary information, and commitment with Māori people group add to a socially educated way to deal with safeguarding this jeopardized species. This reconciliation advances preservation methodologies as well as perceives the significance of native insight in forming successful ecological administration.

Difficulties and Future Headings: Exploring the Protection Scene:

While New Zealand's drives to safeguard local species and reestablish biological systems have accomplished prominent triumphs, they are not without challenges. Obtrusive species, living space misfortune, and the continuous effects of environmental change present diligent dangers. The fragile harmony between protection endeavors and community to normal spaces requires ceaseless variation and smart administration.

As New Zealand explores the developing protection scene, future bearings remember a concentration for environment versatile preservation techniques, improved coordinated effort with neighborhood networks, and the combination of mechanical developments for checking and the executives. Adjusting to arising difficulties and utilizing the qualities of both customary and contemporary methodologies will be urgent in guaranteeing the drawn out progress of protection drives.

Gatekeepers of Biodiversity and Environments:

In the unpredictable dance of preservation in Aotearoa, New Zealanders arise as gatekeepers of biodiversity and biological systems. The drives to safeguard local species and reestablish biological systems epitomize a promise to protecting the country's normal legacy for a long time into the future. From hunter free goals to local area drove establishing projects, the protection scene mirrors an ensemble of endeavors, each note adding to the strength and essentialness of New Zealand's exceptional biological systems.

As the country proceeds with its excursion as stewards of the land and ocean, the examples gained from these drives swell across the worldwide protection local area. New Zealand's imaginative methodologies, local area commitment, and joining of customary thinking offer important bits of knowledge into the mind boggling errand of shielding biodiversity even with extraordinary difficulties. The tale of safeguarding local species and reestablishing biological systems in Aotearoa isn't simply a story of protection achievement; it is a continuous obligation to fitting the fragile harmony among mankind and the regular world.

8.3 Highlight success stories and ongoing challenges in conservation efforts.

Watchmen of Aotearoa: Exploring Protection Victories and Continuous Difficulties

In the rich embroidery of New Zealand's protection scene, examples of overcoming adversity and progressing difficulties entwine, framing a story that mirrors the country's obligation to defending its remarkable biodiversity. From the thriving resurgence of imperiled species to the determined dangers presented by obtrusive species and natural surroundings debasement, the protection venture in Aotearoa is a dynamic and developing adventure.

Examples of overcoming adversity: An Orchestra of Preservation Wins

1. **The Wonderful Rebound of the Kākāpō:**
   Among the resonating examples of overcoming adversity in New Zealand's preservation endeavors is the striking rebound of the kākāpō, a basically imperiled parrot. With its unmistakable emerald-green plumage and charming character, the kākāpō confronted impending annihilation. Through serious preservation measures, including territory security, hunter control, and a painstakingly overseen hostage reproducing program, the kākāpō populace has encountered a resurgence. The deliberate endeavors of moderates and the commitment of the Division of Preservation (DOC) have pushed the kākāpō from the verge of insensibility to an encouraging sign for jeopardized species recuperation.

2. **Whio For eternity: Defending the Blue Duck:**
   The Whio Perpetually program remains as a demonstration of the fruitful protection of the whio, or blue duck. This remarkable waterfowl, endemic

to New Zealand's quick streaming waterways, confronted dangers from presented hunters and living space debasement. The cooperative endeavors of the DOC, neighborhood iwi (clans), and networks have renewed whio populaces. Preservation drives, directed by Mātauranga Māori (customary information), have safeguarded the species as well as highlighted the meaning of native insight in viable natural stewardship. The resurgence of the whio represents the force of local area commitment and a comprehensive way to deal with preservation.

3. **Rebuilding of Ōtuataua Stonefields:**
The rebuilding of Ōtuataua Stonefields in South Auckland addresses a victory in saving social and biological legacy. This generally critical site, including antiquated magma fields and archeological remainders, confronted dangers from metropolitan turn of events. Through cooperative endeavors including nearby networks, iwi, and preservation associations, the stonefields have been reestablished to their regular state. Local vegetation has been once again introduced, and the site presently fills in as a living demonstration of the agreeable concurrence of social and natural qualities. The outcome of Ōtuataua Stonefields exhibits the potential for coordinating social legacy conservation with biological rebuilding.

4. **Kaikōura Marine Watchmen: Safeguarding Maritime Wealth:**
The Kaikōura Marine Watchmen embody fruitful local area drove preservation endeavors in shielding marine biological systems. The Hikurangi Marine Save, laid out in 2014 with the direction of neighborhood networks and iwi, has turned into a sanctuary for marine life. From dynamic coral networks to different fish species, the hold exhibits the regenerative capability of very much oversaw marine protection regions. The Kaikōura Marine Watchmen's obligation to dependable the travel industry and maintainable practices features the significance of local area stewardship in safeguarding New Zealand's valuable waterfront conditions.

5. **The Renewed introduction of Kiwi to Ōhope Grand Hold:**

The Ōhope Grand Save on the North Island saw an achievement in protection with the effective renewed introduction of kiwi, New Zealand's notorious flightless bird. Kiwi, when near the very edge of decline because of predation by presented vertebrates, have found a shelter in hunter controlled regions. The coordinated effort between the Whakatāne Kiwi Trust, neighborhood networks, and the DOC has empowered the foundation of a place of refuge for kiwi. The sound of kiwi calls reverberating through the save represents the outcome of designated preservation endeavors in giving a future to these significant birds.

Progressing Difficulties: Exploring the Protection Scene

1. **Intrusive Species: The Enduring Danger:**
In spite of remarkable triumphs, obtrusive species stay a steady test in New Zealand's preservation scene. Presented hunters like rodents, stoats, and possums keep on presenting huge dangers to local widely varied vegetation. The fight against these trespassers requires continuous endeavors in bother control, imaginative catching advances, and local area commitment. The Hunter Free New Zealand 2050 drive, while aggressive, highlights the extent of the test. Adjusting the requirement for successful vermin control with moral contemplations and the intricacy of metropolitan conditions stays a continuous riddle in the preservation story.

2. **Natural surroundings Misfortune and Discontinuity: The Effect of Advancement:**
As New Zealand encounters urbanization and foundation advancement, living space misfortune and discontinuity arise as basic difficulties. Local biological systems face tension from land-use changes, influencing the network and practicality of territories. Protection drives should explore the fragile harmony among improvement and safeguarding, underlining the significance of reasonable land-use rehearses. The rebuilding of biodiversity passageways and the foundation of central area islands become vital systems in relieving the effects of natural surroundings misfortune and fracture.

3. **Environmental Change: Capricious Fates:**
The phantom of environmental change adds a layer of intricacy to New Zealand's protection challenges. Climbing temperatures, outrageous climate occasions, and moving environmental examples request versatile techniques. Species that are especially powerless against environmental change, like those ward on unambiguous temperature systems, face unsure prospects. Preservation endeavors should integrate environment strength, perceiving the interconnectedness of natural frameworks and the requirement for adaptable administration draws near. The continuous checking and appraisal of environment influences on biodiversity become basic parts of protection arranging.

4. **Kauri Dieback Sickness: A Quiet Danger to Old Goliaths:**
The determination of kauri dieback sickness represents a remarkable test in the protection mosaic. Kauri trees, old goliaths that have molded New Zealand's scenes for quite a long time, are in danger of capitulating to a minute microbe. The executives endeavors include track terminations, cleanliness stations, and investigation into sickness safe kauri. The fragile harmony between community to see the value in these old trees and the basic to shield them from the gamble of sickness transmission highlights the nuanced idea of protection navigation.

5. **Human-Natural life Struggle: Adjusting Protection and Human Exercises:**
   As preservation endeavors endeavor to safeguard local species, clashes with human exercises, especially in metropolitan and peri-metropolitan regions, become evident. Local birds settling in neighborhoods might confront dangers from homegrown pets, and protection objectives might conflict with improvement plans. Accomplishing an amicable harmony among preservation and human exercises requires creative arrangements, local area schooling, and cooperative direction. Exploring this sensitive balance stays a continuous test in the preservation account.

6. **Subsidizing and Asset Imperatives: Supporting Protection Force:**

The monetary and asset requirements on protection drives present continuous difficulties. While there is a common obligation to natural protection, getting subsidizing for long haul projects and keeping up with the energy of preservation endeavors can be problematic. Preservation associations, frequently dependent on a mix of government backing, generosity, and public gifts, wrestle with the requirement for economical subsidizing models. Adjusting transient financial plan limitations with the basic for long haul biological flexibility stays a powerful test in the preservation scene.

The Ensemble Proceeds: A Unique Preservation Story

As New Zealand explores the perplexing dance of protection victories and progressing difficulties, the story keeps on unfurling. Every example of overcoming adversity is a demonstration of the devotion of moderates, the flexibility of local species, and the force of local area commitment. At the same time, the difficulties highlight the requirement for versatile systems, insightful direction, and an all encompassing comprehension of the interconnected variables molding New Zealand's natural future.

In the ensemble of Aotearoa's preservation endeavors, the songs of wins and difficulties blend to make a powerful story. The continuous obligation to safeguarding local species and saving biological systems mirrors an aggregate ethos of guardianship. As the watchmen of Aotearoa, New Zealanders explore the complicated protection scene, endeavoring to guarantee that the rich embroidered artwork of biodiversity stays lively for a long time into the future. The ensemble proceeds, a demonstration of the strength of nature and the getting through obligation to stewardship in the place that is known for the long white cloud.

CHAPTER 9

"A Kiwi's Journey"

A Kiwi's Excursion: Exploring the Rich Embroidery of New Zealand's Scene and Culture

In the core of the South Pacific lies a place that is known for charm and marvel — a spot known as Aotearoa, the Place that is known for the Long White Cloud. Here the kiwi, both the famous flightless bird and the charming term for Another Zealander, leaves on an excursion through a different and enamoring scene, woven with the strings of culture, nature, and experience. As we follow the kiwi's excursion, we dive into the remarkable embroidery of New Zealand's encounters, from the lavish plant life of Fiordland to the dynamic Maori culture, catching the embodiment of a country that entices voyagers and visionaries the same.

Setting out on the Kiwi's Path: An Embroidery of Scenes

1. **Fiordland: Where Vegetation Unfurls Like a Story:**
   Our process starts in Fiordland, a great locale on the southwestern tip of the South Island. Here, the kiwi experiences lavish, old woods, where transcending trees like the rimu and totara make a green embroidery that appears to unfurl like a story.
   Fiordland's notable coves, for example, Milford Sound and Suspicious Sound, feature nature's glory — a demonstration of the mind boggling handicraft of glacial masses and the chiseling dash of time. As the kiwi crosses the greenery covered valleys and dim scenes, it becomes submerged in reality as we know it where each corner uncovers another part in the account of New Zealand's normal marvels.

2. **Southern Alps: Pinnacles that Murmur Stories of Experience:**
   Leaving the tranquility of Fiordland, our kiwi takes off toward the north, arriving at the imposing Southern Alps. Here, snow-covered tops intersperse the horizon, murmuring stories of experience and testing the bold soul. Aoraki/Mount Cook, New Zealand's most noteworthy pinnacle,

remains as a sentinel, welcoming brave voyagers to investigate its elevated paths and icy masses. As the kiwi steps the high country ways, it experiences a steadily changing scene — an orchestra of rock, ice, and sky that catches the pith of New Zealand's standing as the experience capital of the world.

3. Rotorua: Revealing the Geothermal Material:

Proceeding with its excursion, our kiwi shows up in Rotorua, a district on the North Island where the world's geothermal heartbeat beats underneath the surface. Here, the scene turns into a material painted with striking geothermal tints — bubbling mud pools, emitting fountains, and steaming natural aquifers. The kiwi observes the basic powers that shape the land, an indication of the dynamic and consistently developing nature of Aotearoa. In Rotorua, the kiwi encounters the geothermal miracles as well as drenches itself in the rich Maori social embroidered artwork that characterizes the area.

Drenching in Maori Culture: Strings of Custom and Otherworldliness

1. **Te Whakarewarewa: Living Among the Geothermal Watchmen:**
   As the kiwi investigates Rotorua, it experiences Te Whakarewarewa, a living Maori town settled in the midst of the geothermal miracles. Here, the strings of Maori custom mesh flawlessly into the scene. The kiwi observes the glow of the nearby local area, who have agreeably existed together with the geothermal powers for ages. The conventional Maori design, enhanced with mind boggling carvings and representative examples, recounts accounts of progenitors and otherworldly associations with the land. The kiwi turns into a member in the social haka, a strong dance that repeats the flexibility and strength of the Maori public.

2. **Wharenui and Wharekai: Corridors of Custom and Friendliness:**
   In the core of Maori culture, the kiwi enters the consecrated space of the wharenui, the gathering house. Enhanced with intricate carvings and dynamic craftsmanship, the wharenui is a vault of hereditary stories and profound importance. As the kiwi ventures inside, it feels the tangible association with the customs that have molded the Maori lifestyle.
   Contiguous the wharenui is the wharekai, the common feasting lobby, where the kiwi participates in the sharing of kai (food) and encounters the pith of Maori cordiality. Through the ceremonies of koha (gift-giving) and the sharing of stories, the kiwi turns into a fundamental piece of the social trade that characterizes Maori neighborliness.

3. **Waiata and Kapa Haka: Reverberations of Social Articulation:**

As the kiwi proceeds with its excursion through Maori culture, it experiences the cadenced hints of waiata (melodies) and kapa haka (performing expressions). These types of social articulation are the strings that associate ages, telling stories of adoration, misfortune, win, and solidarity. The kiwi ends up encompassed by the full voices and synchronized developments that are the heartbeat of Maori culture. Through waiata and kapa haka, the kiwi encounters the spirit blending magnificence of a culture that celebrates the two its old customs and its energetic contemporary articulations.

Nature's Range: Investigating the Assorted Scenes of Aotearoa

1. **Marlborough Sounds: Beach front Quietness and Biodiversity:**
   Leaving the social hug of Rotorua, the kiwi adventures north to the Marlborough Sounds, a seaside heaven at the tip of the South Island. Here, the scene advances from geothermal marvels to peaceful streams and lavish slopes. The kiwi investigates the complex organization of sounds, where the gathering of land and ocean makes a sanctuary for marine life. In the midst of the local bramble, the kiwi experiences birdlife remarkable to the district, including the tricky kiwi bird itself — a sign of the sensitive harmony among safeguarding and investigation that characterizes New Zealand's preservation endeavors.

2. **Abel Tasman Public Park: Brilliant Sea shores and Beach front Paths:**
   As the kiwi wanders along the northern bank of the South Island, it finds the brilliant sea shores and turquoise waters of Abel Tasman Public Park. This beach front jewel is embellished with an organization of strolling trails that breeze through local hedge and deal stunning vistas of the Tasman Ocean. The kiwi, with its unmistakable feeling of interest, investigates the secret bays and flowing estuaries, experiencing the different verdure that flourish in this beach front shelter. Abel Tasman turns into a material painted with the shades of the sea, the verdant woodlands, and the brilliant sands — a demonstration of the regular magnificence that characterizes Aotearoa.

3. **Coromandel Landmass: Unconventional Sea shores and Kauri Backwoods:**

Our kiwi's process takes a toward the east go to the Coromandel Landmass, a district known for its unusual sea shores, rough shoreline, and old kauri timberlands. Here, the kiwi experiences the famous Heated Water Ocean side, where warm action underneath the sands permits guests to dig their own hot pools.

The kiwi digs into the rich kauri woodlands, where transcending trees give testimony regarding hundreds of years of progress. The perplexing harmony among land and ocean, between geothermal marvels and flawless sea shores, unfurls as the kiwi drenches itself in the different scenes of the Coromandel.

Experience Calls: Investigating the Adventures of the Experience Capital

1. **Queenstown: Where Adrenaline Meets High Magnificence:**
   As our kiwi process changes toward the South Island's inside, it shows up in Queenstown — the undisputed experience capital of New Zealand. Encircled by the Southern Alps and settled on the shores of Lake Wakatipu, Queenstown is a jungle gym where adrenaline meets high magnificence. The kiwi feels the surge of energy as it thinks about bungee hopping from the notable Kawarau Extension, the origin of this really considering adventuring. With the Remarkables mountain range as a background, Queenstown turns into a shelter for daredevils, offering exercises from skydiving to fly drifting. The kiwi, with its brave soul, embraces the heartbeating appeal of Queenstown.

2. **Wanaka: Peaceful Lakes and Mountain Vistas:**

   A short excursion from Queenstown takes our kiwi to Wanaka, a town settled on the shores of Lake Wanaka. Here, experience takes an interruption, and quietness turns into the hero. The kiwi investigates the tranquil lake, encompassed by snow-covered tops and high glades. Roys Pinnacle Track offers an all encompassing vista that stretches across the Southern Alps, welcoming examination and reflection. Wanaka turns into a relief, where the kiwi, in the midst of the normal magnificence, tracks down a harmony between the excitement of experience and the peacefulness of nature.

Culinary Odyssey: Examining the Kinds of Aotearoa

1. **Te Wai Pounamu: A Gastronomic Excursion in the South Island:**
   Our kiwi, having navigated different scenes and embraced social encounters, presently leaves on a culinary odyssey. In Te Wai Pounamu, the South Island, it experiences the kinds of a gastronomic scene formed by nearby produce and social impacts. The kiwi enjoys the newness of Feign shellfish, famous for their briny pleasantness, and enjoys the deliciousness of Fiordland venison — a demonstration of New Zealand's obligation to supportable and moral cultivating rehearses. The rich embroidery of Te Wai Pounamu's culinary scene is woven with the strings of custom and development, mirroring a promise to quality fixings and a festival of neighborhood flavors.

2. **Te Ika-a-Māui: North Island's Culinary Variety:**

Crossing the Cook Waterway, our kiwi shows up in Te Ika-a-Māui, the North Island, where an embroidery of culinary variety unfurls. In Wellington, the kiwi investigates Cuba Road, an energetic center of bistros, diners, and culinary imagination.

Here, the kiwi gets a kick out of the combination of worldwide impacts and the creative turns on customary Kiwi toll. Moving north to Hawke's Inlet, known for its honor winning wineries and plantations, the kiwi encounters a gala of flavors — craftsman cheeses, delicious organic products, and top notch wines. Te Ika-a-Māui turns into a sense of taste satisfying excursion, where the kiwi finds the lavishness of New Zealand's culinary legacy.

A Kiwi's Appearance on Aotearoa's Abundance

As our kiwi finishes up its excursion through the different scenes, social fortunes, and audacious quests for Aotearoa, it considers the rich woven art- work that characterizes New Zealand. From the unblemished sea shores of the Coromandel to the adrenaline-siphoning encounters of Queenstown, from the social energy of Rotorua to the peaceful scenes of Wanaka, Aotearoa unfurls as a place that is known for differences and harmonies.

The kiwi, both the flightless bird and the epitome of the Kiwi soul, ends up interweaved with the strings of custom, nature, and experience. It has investi- gated the geothermal miracles of Rotorua, took off through the Southern Alps, and appreciated the different kinds of Kiwi food. It has moved to the rhythms of Maori waiata, embraced the excitement of Queenstown's experiences, and tracked down comfort in the quiet magnificence of Wanaka.

In the embroidery of Aotearoa, the kiwi finds an actual excursion as well as a profound one — an excursion that rises above scenes and embraces the embodiment of being Kiwi. It conveys with it the narratives of the land, the reverberations of social articulation, and the dauntless soul of experience. As the kiwi's process finishes up, it abandons impressions in the sands of Boiling Water Ocean side, reverberations of haka in the wharenui, and recollections of snow capped vistas in the Southern Alps.

Aotearoa, with its different scenes and social wealth, entices explorers and local people the same to drench themselves in the excellence of the Long White Cloud. The kiwi, having navigated mountains and waterways, social practices and culinary pleasures, remains as an image of the aggregate excursion — an excursion that commends the phenomenal abundance of Aotearoa and the soul of the individuals who call it home.

9.1 Conclude the book with a reflection on the author's personal journey through the Green Isles and Blue Waters of New Zealand.

Epilog: An Individual Reflection on the Green Isles and Blue Waters of Aotearoa

As I pen down the last lines of this story, I wind up submerged in an embroidery woven with the strings of investigation, revelation, and genuine association — a woven artwork that reflects not just the different scenes of the Green Isles and Blue Waters of New Zealand yet in addition the reverberations of an individual excursion that rises above the pages of this book.

Aotearoa, with its charming excellence and energetic soul, has been in excess of a subject of investigation; it has turned into a material whereupon my own encounters have been painted, each stroke uncovering layers of association and revelation.

Setting out on the Odyssey: An Excursion of Words and Ponders

The excursion through the Green Isles and Blue Waters started not with strides on Kiwi soil but rather with the transform of pages and the submersion into stories turned by others. The expressions of writers, the narratives of explorers, and the reverberations of native insight painted clear pictures in my brain — a preface to the odyssey that anticipated. As I dove into the stories of the rich Fiordland, the snow-covered pinnacles of the Southern Alps, and the geothermal miracles of Rotorua, a feeling of expectation and marvel encouraged inside me. Much to my dismay that these words would before long change into lived encounters, and the scenes they depicted would turn into the scenery of my own excursion.

The Green Isles Disclosed: Investigating the Different Scenes

The lavish scenes of New Zealand, suitably depicted as the Green Isles, unfurled before me like a fantasy. The tough excellence of Fiordland, with its flowing cascades and old woodlands, turned into a reality as I remained on the shores of Milford Sound, encompassed by the foggy greatness of nature. The Southern Alps, a grand embroidery of snow and rock, moved me to rise their pinnacles and witness the world from their elevated vantage point. The geothermal miracles of Rotorua, with their percolating mud pools and ejecting fountains, became a portrayal in a book as well as a tactile encounter, where the world's pulse reverberated through each step.

As I followed the kiwi's excursion through Abel Tasman Public Park, the Coromandel Promontory, and the Marlborough Sounds, I wound up remaining on brilliant sea shores, investigating old kauri woodlands, and exploring the multifaceted streams that characterize the waterfront quietness of Aotearoa. The different scenes turned into a jungle gym for the faculties, every area making a permanent imprint on my memory. From the serenity of Wanaka's lake shores to the experience loaded Queenstown, I embraced the differentiations and harmonies that make New Zealand an embroidery of unmatched excellence.

Blue Waters Calling: Drenching in Marine Marvels

The Blue Waters of New Zealand, extending from the Tasman Ocean to the Pacific Sea, enticed with commitments of marine marvels and waterfront quality. The perfect sea shores of the Coromandel, with their unconventional magnificence, turned into a position of comfort and reflection. The marine life that occupies the waters around Aotearoa — from whales and dolphins to the special yellow-looked at penguins — dazzled my creative mind, welcoming me to observe their effortlessness and strength. In investigating the marine domains, I experienced the wealth of biodiversity as well as seen the fragile harmony between preservation endeavors and the intrinsic appeal of the sea.

Social Odyssey: Disentangling Maori Fantasies and Legends

The social odyssey through the Green Isles uncovered the profundities of Maori fantasies and legends, welcoming me to investigate the complexities of Te Ao Māori — the Maori world. From the living customs of Te Whakarewarewa to the enamoring waiata and kapa haka exhibitions, I saw the significant association between the Maori public and the land. The wharenui and wharekai became designs of wood and carvings as well as vessels of social progression and local area meeting. As I dove into the rich Mātauranga Māori, the reconciliation of native insight into protection endeavors and social practices turned into a wellspring of motivation, underlining the comprehensive way to deal with natural stewardship.

Experience Capital and Culinary Pleasures: Enjoying the Kiwi Soul

Queenstown, hailed as the experience capital of the world, ended up being in excess of a center for adrenaline-siphoning exercises. It turned into a similitude for the Kiwi soul — an epitome of valor, investigation, and a profound association with the land. Bungee bouncing from the Kawarau Scaffold wasn't simply an experience; it was a representative jump into the soul of Aotearoa. Wanaka, with its peaceful lakes and mountain vistas, gave a differentiation — an update that the Kiwi soul embraces both the excitement of experience and the tranquility of nature.

The culinary excursion through New Zealand unfurled as a festival of flavors and customs. From the newness of Feign shellfish to the craftsman cheeses of Hawke's Narrows, each dish turned into a demonstration of the abundance of Aotearoa's territory and ocean. The combination of worldwide impacts in Wellington's Cuba Road reflected the multicultural embroidery of New Zealand's general public, where various culinary customs mix into an exceptional Kiwi flavor. Food turned into a focal point through which I associated with the cooking as well as with the tales of individuals who develop, plan, and offer these culinary joys.

Preservation Narratives: Exploring the Sensitive Equilibrium

The investigation of New Zealand's obligation to natural preservation gave bits of knowledge into the sensitive harmony among insurance and access. The drives to safeguard local species, reestablish environments, and connect with networks in protection endeavors featured the country's devotion to shielding its regular legacy. The difficulties presented by intrusive species, living space misfortune, environmental change, and the sensitive dance between experience the travel industry and ecological protection highlighted the nuanced choices that shape New Zealand's preservation scene.

Kiwi Cordiality: Accounts of Associations and Warmth

In the midst of the scenes and social ponders, the warm and inviting nature of the Kiwi public arose as a subject woven into the texture of my excursion. The tales of voyagers interfacing with local people, the liberality of cordiality in networks, and the certified warmth reached out to those investigating the Green Isles made a story of shared humankind.

The idea of manaakitanga — a Maori esteem underscoring cordiality, generosity, and care — became a social quality as well as a core value that characterized my connections and encounters.

Reflections on the Excursion: An Embroidery of Appreciation

As I consider this individual excursion through the Green Isles and Blue Waters of New Zealand, appreciation wells inside me — a profound appreciation for the snapshots of marvel, the associations manufactured, and the examples learned. The scenes, whether covered in fog in Fiordland or washed in brilliant daylight in the Coromandel, have engraved themselves on my spirit. The social lavishness, from the unpredictable carvings of a wharenui to the harmonies of a waiata, has turned into a tune that resounds inside me.

The experiences with marine life, the surge of experience, the kinds of Kiwi cooking, and the glow of neighborliness have on the whole laid out a picture of Aotearoa — a representation that goes past the actual excellence and digs into the core of the country. The kiwi, with its emblematic flightlessness and its job as the moniker for New Zealanders, has turned into a friend in this excursion — an encapsulation of versatility, interest, and the persevering through soul that characterizes Aotearoa.

In navigating the Green Isles and Blue Waters, I have not just noticed; I have partaken in a living story. The protection endeavors, social customs, and the entwining of nature and mankind have made a permanent imprint on how I might interpret being a steward of the Earth. The sensitive dance among safeguarding and investigation, the concordance among custom and advancement, and the festival of variety have turned into the core values of my own excursion.

Aotearoa, an Embroidery of Congruity and Change

As I close this individual reflection, I observe that Aotearoa isn't simply an objective on a guide; it is an embroidery woven with strings of congruity and change. It is where old scenes coincide with current desires, where social customs persevere close by contemporary articulations. The Green Isles and Blue Waters have turned into an illustration for the powerful interaction of safeguarding and progress, custom and development — an embroidery that recounts an account of a country that embraces its past while graphing a course for what's to come.

In this excursion, I have become a spectator as well as a member in the continuous story of Aotearoa. The scenes and social fortunes have formed the pages of this book as well as the parts of my own story. As I bid goodbye to the Green Isles and Blue Waters, I convey with me recollections as well as a significant feeling of association with a land that has uncovered its entire being.

May the reverberations of the Southern Alps, the murmurs of the coves, and the rhythms of the haka wait in the pages of this story. May the narratives of protection endeavors, the glow of Kiwi accommodation, and the kinds of culinary pleasures keep on resounding. What's more, as the kiwi, both bird and soul, stays an image of versatility, interest, and association, may the embroidery of Aotearoa persevere — an immortal story that welcomes all who adventure into its folds to turn out to be important for the continuous excursion through the Green Isles and Blue Waters of New Zealand.

9.2 Encourage readers to embark on their own adventures and explore the wonders of Aotearoa.

Greeting to Experience: Set out on Your Aotearoa Odyssey

As the pages of this story turn, arranging distinctive scenes and social embroideries, I broaden a sincere greeting — a solicitation to you, dear peruser, to set out on your own odyssey through the charming marvels of Aotearoa, the Place that is known for the Long White Cloud. Past the bounds of this text lies a world ready to be investigated, a reality where the Green Isles and Blue Waters entice with an ensemble of regular miracles, social fortunes, and undertakings that mix the spirit.

A Material of Different Scenes: Reveal the Magnificence of Aotearoa

Start your process by disentangling the material of assorted scenes that characterizes the Green Isles of New Zealand. Imagine yourself remaining on the shores of Milford Sound, where fog covered inlets cut their direction through old backwoods, making a permanent imprint on your faculties. Feel the smash of snow underneath your boots as you climb the Southern Alps, where all encompassing vistas and high greatness anticipate the individuals who try to wander. Envision the glow of Rotorua's geothermal hug, where foaming mud pools and emitting fountains paint a clear representation of the World's crude power. The Green Isles, with their lavish vegetation and sensational geography, anticipate your impressions — a material prepared for the strokes of your own investigation.

Submerge in Maori Culture: Dance to the Rhythms of Custom

Let the reverberations of Maori culture entice you into an existence where fantasies and legends are scratched into the actual texture of the land. Imagine yourself in Te Whakarewarewa, a residing Maori town settled in the midst of geothermal miracles, where social customs mix with the powers of nature. Step inside the wharenui, the hallowed gathering house embellished with unpredictable carvings, and feel the tribal stories show signs of life. Participate in the cadenced dance of the haka, where the strength and soul of the Maori public are commended through strong developments and reminiscent serenades. In

Aotearoa, the Maori culture welcomes you not exclusively to notice however to take part — to move, to sing, and to turn out to be essential professionally embroidery that traverses ages.

Nature's Orchestra: From Fiordland to the Coromandel

As you cross the different scenes of Aotearoa, permit nature's orchestra to entertain you. Envision the delicate lapping of water in the Marlborough Sounds, where seaside tranquility meets biodiversity in an agreeable dance. Imagine yourself meandering through Abel Tasman Public Park, where brilliant sea shores and turquoise waters make a beach front heaven. Feel the capricious breeze on the Coromandel Promontory, where boiling water springs meet immaculate sea shores, offering a special mix of geothermal miracles and beach front magnificence. The ensemble of Aotearoa is made out of stirring leaves, hurrying water, and the calls of local birds — a song that reverberates through every special scene, welcoming you to be a piece of its charming structure.

Experience Is standing by: Queenstown's Rushes and Wanaka's Serenity

For the energetic traveler inside you, the Green Isles unfurl as a jungle gym where adrenaline meets high greatness. Envision yourself in Queenstown, the experience capital of the world, remaining on the memorable Kawarau Scaffold, prepared to bring the jump into a universe of elating bungee hops and heart-beating encounters. Feel the rush as you take off through the Southern Alps, whether on a skydiving venture or a fly drifting experience on Lake Wakatipu. What's more, when the rush dies down, track down comfort in Wanaka, where quiet lakes and mountain vistas make a shelter for reflection and peacefulness. The Green Isles offer a range of encounters — from the beat reviving to the spirit mitigating — guaranteeing that experience anticipates every step of the way.

Culinary Joys: A Gastronomic Excursion through Kiwi Flavors

No excursion through Aotearoa is finished without a culinary odyssey that entices the taste buds. Envision yourself relishing the newness of Feign clams in Te Wai Pounamu, the South Island, or enjoying the deliciousness of Fiordland venison — a demonstration of New Zealand's obligation to supportable and moral cultivating rehearses. Cross the North Island's culinary variety, investigating the lively restaurants of Wellington's Cuba Road and savoring the craftsman cheeses and elite wines of Hawke's Sound. Allow your sense of taste to be your aide as you explore the rich embroidery of New Zealand's culinary scene, where new and neighborhood fixings wind around together to make a gastronomic ensemble.

Protection Narratives: Be a Watchman of Aotearoa's Biodiversity

As you dig into the Green Isles and Blue Waters, become a watchman of Aotearoa's biodiversity. Imagine yourself adding to preservation endeavors, whether by chipping in local tree establishing drives or supporting associations committed to safeguarding jeopardized species. Embrace the sensitive harmony between experience the travel industry and ecological preservation, proceeding with caution on the land while partaking in the excitement of investigation. Aotearoa's obligation to ecological stewardship welcomes you to be a functioning member in the continuous story of protection — a story where each individual can have an effect in saving the normal magnificence of this extraordinary land.

Kiwi Cordiality: Interface with the Core of Aotearoa

Past the scenes and experiences, the glow of Kiwi neighborliness makes the excursion genuinely remarkable. Imagine yourself associating with local people, sharing stories, and encountering the veritable benevolence that characterizes manaakitanga — the soul of friendliness in Maori culture. Whether you wind up in a little beach front town or a clamoring metropolitan focus, the Kiwi public greet you wholeheartedly, welcoming you to turn out to be important for their local area. Let the accounts of voyagers' encounters and associations with local people motivate you to manufacture your own significant associations, making recollections that wait long after you've left the shores of Aotearoa.

Your Odyssey Starts: Embrace the Soul of the Kiwi

As you consider the Green Isles and Blue Waters of Aotearoa, know that this story is a greeting, an enticing call to leave on your own odyssey through the marvels of New Zealand. Whether you are attracted to the unblemished sea shores of the Coromandel, the rough magnificence of Fiordland, or the social lavishness of Rotorua, the soul of the Kiwi anticipates your disclosure. This is a chance to submerge yourself in the scenes that have blended the hearts of wayfarers for quite a long time, to move to the rhythms of Maori culture, and to taste the kinds of Kiwi cooking.

Gather your sacks with a feeling of interest, strength, and experience. Permit the Green Isles and Blue Waters to be the background of your own accounts, each stage a brushstroke on the material of your own excursion. Embrace the opportunity to investigate, to interface, and to be changed by the miracles that Aotearoa unfurls before you. The kiwi, with its emblematic flightlessness and lively disposition, becomes a bird as well as a buddy in your investigation — an aide through the scenes and social fortunes that characterize the Place that is known for the Long White Cloud.

As you set out on your Aotearoa odyssey, may the scenes rouse wonderment, the social encounters encourage understanding, and the experiences touch off the excitement of revelation. In the Green Isles and Blue Waters, you will find an objective as well as an embroidery of encounters ready to be woven into the texture of your own story. Embrace the soul of the Kiwi, embrace the soul of Aotearoa, and let your process be a demonstration of the vast miracles that anticipate the individuals who look to investigate the essence of New Zealand.

9.3 Provide practical tips for travelers, including sustainable practices and cultural sensitivity.

Exploring Aotearoa: Reasonable Tips for Economical and Socially Reasonable Travel

Leaving on an excursion through the Green Isles and Blue Waters of Aotearoa isn't just about investigation — a pledge to dependable travel regards the climate and praises the rich social legacy of New Zealand.

As you get ready for your experience, consider these reasonable tips that go past the common travel guide, offering bits of knowledge into maintainable practices and social aversion to guarantee a significant and deferential investigation of this delightful land.

1. **Embrace Manageable Travel Practices:**
   Aotearoa's immaculate scenes entice voyagers to proceed with caution and embrace maintainable practices. Consider picking eco-accommodating convenience choices that focus on natural protection. Many cabins and lodgings in New Zealand are focused on limiting their carbon impression and advancing mindful the travel industry. Also, investigate transportation choices, for example, electric or mixture vehicles to lessen your effect on the climate. New Zealand's deeply grounded organization of strolling trails gives a superb chance to submerge yourself in nature without leaving a critical environmental impression.

2. **Interface with Neighborhood Protection Drives:**
   Take part in neighborhood protection endeavors to effectively add to safeguarding New Zealand's exceptional biodiversity. Various drives and volunteer projects welcome explorers to participate in exercises, for example, tree planting, territory reclamation, and natural life observing. By turning into an involved member in protection projects, you not just add to the security of Aotearoa's normal ponders yet additionally gain a more profound comprehension of the fragile harmony among safeguarding and investigation.

3. **Regard the Maori Social Legacy:**
   Aotearoa's character is profoundly interwoven with Maori culture, and as a guest, moving toward it with deference and social sensitivity is fundamental. Get to know essential Maori customs, like the customary hello, the hongi (squeezing noses together). While visiting Marae (Maori meeting grounds), be aware of social conventions, including taking off your shoes and looking for consent prior to taking photos. Understanding the meaning of social practices improves your experience and cultivates a more significant association with the native legacy of New Zealand.

4. **Become familiar with a Couple of Expressions of Te Reo Maori:**
   Te Reo Maori, the Maori language, is a critical part of New Zealand's social character. While numerous Kiwis are conversant in English, really trying to learn and utilize essential Maori good tidings and expressions

shows social regard. Basic good tidings like "Kia ora" (hi) and "Haere ra" (farewell) can go quite far in encouraging positive cooperations with local people. Embracing the language mirrors a guarantee to social drenching and appreciation.

5. **Look for Consent for Photography:**
   While catching the stunning scenes and social encounters of Aotearoa, be thoughtful and look for consent prior to shooting individuals, particularly in socially delicate settings. This signal recognizes the security and social practices of the people you experience. In specific areas, photography might be confined or restricted to safeguard the profound meaning of the site. Continuously stick to signage and direction given by nearby specialists.

6. **Support Nearby People group:**
   Add to the prosperity of neighborhood networks by supporting nearby organizations, craftsmans, and makers. Investigate ranchers' business sectors, make fairs, and shop stores to buy real, privately made keepsakes. Drawing in with nearby networks cultivates financial manageability as well as gives potential chances to find out about the special stories and customs of the districts you visit.

7. **Practice Capable Untamed life Survey:**
   Aotearoa is home to different and remarkable natural life, including intriguing and imperiled species. While participating in untamed life seeing exercises, focus on mindful and moral practices. Pick visit administrators and exercises that comply with moral rules, guaranteeing negligible unsettling influence to regular environments and natural life. Maintain a conscious separation and cease from taking care of or contacting wild creatures. Capable untamed life the travel industry adds to the protection of New Zealand's normal fortunes.

8. **Remain Informed About Open air Morals:**
   Whether you're climbing in Fiordland Public Park or kayaking in the Abel Tasman, it is vital to remain informed about open air morals. Find out about the standards of "Leave No Follow," which advocate for dependable open air diversion. Pack out all waste, remain on assigned trails, and try not to upset widely varied vegetation. New Zealand's remarkable environments are sensitive, and capable outside rehearses are fundamental to guarantee the safeguarding of its regular excellence.

9. **Find out about Kiwi Customs:**
   Notwithstanding Maori customs, understanding general Kiwi customs upgrades your social mindfulness. Kiwis are known for their cordial and easygoing nature. Take part in easygoing discussions, be available to making new companions, and embrace the casual environment. New

Zealanders esteem lowliness and realness, so go ahead and express your interest in the neighborhood lifestyle.

10. **Be Aware of New Zealand's Climate:**
Aotearoa's weather conditions can be capricious, with conditions fluctuating among areas and seasons. Pack layers and be ready for unexpected changes, particularly assuming that you intend to investigate both the North and South Islands. Precipitation is normal in specific regions, so it is fitting to have waterproof stuff. Really looking at neighborhood weather conditions estimates and being versatile to changing circumstances guarantees a more agreeable and pleasant excursion.

11. **Focus on Wellbeing and Security:**
New Zealand is eminent for its open air exercises, from climbing to water sports. Focus on your wellbeing and security by complying with security rules, wearing proper stuff, and looking for data about likely perils. Whether you're investigating volcanic scenes or wandering into the wild, understanding and regarding wellbeing measures add to a protected and charming travel insight.

12. **Take part in Widespread developments and Celebrations:**

Submerge yourself in the energetic social scene of Aotearoa by going to neighborhood occasions and celebrations. From Maori expressions celebrations to food and wine festivities, these occasions offer a window into the powerful social scene of New Zealand. Partaking in social celebrations improves your movement experience as well as supports the protection and advancement of social customs.

Making a Significant Excursion

As you set out on your excursion through the Green Isles and Blue Waters of Aotearoa, recollect that each step is a potential chance to add to the protection of this novel objective. Manageable practices and social responsiveness structure the establishment for an excursion that investigates as well as regards the regular and social miracles of New Zealand. By embracing these functional tips, you guarantee a dependable travel insight as well as turned into a steward of Aotearoa's magnificence — a wonder that coaxes you to investigate with love, interest, and a promise to leaving a positive effect on the Place that is known for the Long White Cloud.